Palaces

European Palaces

Text by
Reinhard Bentmann &
Heinrich Lickes

translated by
O. Ordish

Cassell
London

Frontispiece:
Vienna, Upper Belvedere: A corner of the
ground-floor garden room (1720–1724), an
apartment intermediate between the interior
and the formally designed gardens, very
typical of baroque palace architecture. The
architect responsible for the overall design of
palace and garden was Prince Eugene's
master builder-in-chief, Johann Lukas von
Hildebrandt (1688–1745), the most import-
ant architect of the Austrian baroque after
Fischer von Erlach.

CASSELL LTD.
35 Red Lion Square, London WC1R 4SG
and at Sydney, Auckland, Toronto, Johannesburg,
an affiliate of
Macmillan Publishing Co., Inc.,
New York

English translation copyright © 1978 Arnoldo Mondadori Company Ltd;
copyright © 1969 by Kodansha Ltd., Tokyo for the illustrations;
copyright © 1977 by Hasso Ebeling Verlag, Luxemburg for the text.

First published in Great Britain 1978

ISBN 0 304 30191 4

Filmset by Keyspools Ltd., Golborne, Lancashire
Printed in Italy by Arnoldo Mondadori Editore, Verona

Contents

Introduction

In about 300 A.D., on the rugged plateau of the Karst near the Dalmatian coast, a region as desolate then as now, the Roman emperor Diocletian ordered a vast architectural construction to be hewn from the living rock and soil. Designed with the strictly axial layout of a Roman military camp interpreted in artistic form, it was intended to symbolize once again the splendour and political might of the already declining Empire. The enormous, hybrid extent of the complex is brought home to the visitor, who can find his way through its ruins only with the help of an archeological guide, by the fact that a complete little modern town, the present-day heart of Split, can nestle inside the palace ruins, much as a whole medieval settlement was housed in the Roman theatre at Nîmes.

Europe had to wait 1,360 years before any comparable undertaking was planned again. By the royal will of Louis XIV the greatest monarch in 17th century Europe, ten thousand workmen, recruited to forced labour in a manner reminiscent of the Pharaohs, were sent to a swampy, sparsely wooded, rather cheerless region some way outside the gates of Paris, hitherto occupied only by a hunting lodge. Here they were employed to wrest from the wilderness a palace and garden that eclipsed all its predecessors and remained for future builders in the grand style a standard and an unattainable ideal. Its name was Versailles.

The palace of Diocletian in modern Split, or Spalato, where the memory of the Roman palace can still be traced in local place names, was not only a palace in the sense of being the official residence of the ruler but in that it fulfilled a widely varied multiplicity of functions, great and small, political, economic, cultural and religious.

What is the literal meaning of the word 'palace'? Current etymology derives it from the Palatine Hill in Rome, on which the Roman emperors had built their great rambling palaces since the days of Augustus Caesar. Like the title 'Caesar', which was later to be transformed into the German *Kaiser*, the Russian *Tsar* and the Persian *Shah*, the name 'palace' pervades the early and later Middle Ages and has been absorbed into our modern vocabulary. The word's modern descendants range from the Carolingian *Kaiser-Pfalz* or Palatinate, through *palas* as the dwelling quarters in a medieval German fortress, to the Italian *palazzo*, the town seat of the ruler or nobility, and finally the French *palais*, now shrunk to the concept of a moderately-sized town house for a titled landowner, to supplement his much larger country estate.

Just as the endless outer walls of Diocletian's palace enclosed all the institutions and offices necessary to the exercise of his dominion, so the extensive grounds of Versailles were the seat of the still more complex functions of a state governed by an absolute monarch.

Common to both these bastions was their physical and psychological distance from the nation's long-established political centre. Three hundred and seventy-five kilometres stretch between Split and the Palatine Hill in Rome. Versailles was nearer its capital: the new palace '*fuori le mura*' lay only 17 kilometres from the old royal residence of the Louvre. But it was sufficiently far away to be untroubled by the transient disturbances and immediate political importunities of the capital city, yet near enough to reach the unstable Parisian mob at short notice and impose law and order.

Why did the rulers so openly withdraw from the parent city, but not settle in a contrasting countryside of natural beauty, choosing instead a dismal area of karst or swamp? One explanation may lie in an artistic principle of classical antiquity (held even by Aristotle and Vitruvius) which persisted into the baroque age: 'by human art to put Nature to shame, to correct and to surpass her'—or, as we more critical and sensitive moderns might say, to overpower her. One can see how that aesthetic assumption would appeal to both late Roman military commander and 17th-century despot as a challenge and test for the authoritarian will to mould and subdue. The very inhospitality of the chosen terrain stimulated the rulers' desire to remake it, to carry the project through against all odds, and by means of architecture and garden design to leave their own ineradicable stamp on the undisciplined chaos of Nature.

But as well as this partial explanation relating to the sovereign's psychology, there were more realistically based political historical and military motives. The castle fortress, an architectural and dominant symbol of medieval power in the landscape, had been rendered obsolete by the invention of long-range artillery. Just as Diocletian, in his Dalmatian palace guarded by mountain ridges, was secure enough to dispense with the heavy fortifications of Rome, so also Louis XIV felt safe enough to renounce the shelter of Paris' protecting walls. His outer line of defence had been pushed back to Vauban's cohesive system of fortifications along the Rhine. Moreover, the king's 'enemies within the gates', the fiercely competitive French nobles, were neither the danger to the crown nor the economic and military threat they had been in the days of the Fronde. For centuries towns and castles had been fortified to hold them in check; now they were content to be stage extras at the court of Versailles.

This 'flight from the town' led, curiously enough, to the immediate founding of a new town. For, just as settlements for the dependents of the medieval castle had grown up around the castle walls, so the royal residence spawned such a quantity of court officials, craftsmen, servants, purveyors and suppliers, that it was soon necessary to plan a well-ordered, almost urban, addition to the palace complex. This was the case not only at Versailles itself but also at some of its German imitations such as Mannheim, Rastatt, Karlsruhe or Arolsen, where often the strictly geometrical plan of the new settlement makes it appear a mere extension of the axial and geometrical principles on which the palace and palace garden themselves were designed.

In fact, this phenomenon was confined neither to Europe nor to the baroque period, but could be observed in all civilizations and times in which comparable authoritarian regimes existed. It was to be seen in the palaces and temple precincts of Ancient Egypt, in the royal seats of ancient India and in pre-Columbian America.

The baroque royal residence, here used strictly in the sense of a palace, was the political powerhouse of absolute rule. It was the seat of legislative and executive authority at a time when the idea of sharing political power was still unfamiliar; when the concentration of legislative, executive and judicial authority vested in a single individual had become a declared national policy. This concentration of initiative so typical of the era is illustrated by the fact that the palace not only functioned as the gathering point of all departments of government in one place, but at the same time represented the setting and stage, the criterion and model of all the cultural and artistic activities of the epoch. In the last analysis, these expressions were used to exalt the concept of central authority and glorify the image of the monarch.

And so the palace, with its indispensable park, served as the appropriate, the rich and highly decorative frame for social display, in which living was turned into ceremonial and an elaborate etiquette controlled every aspect of behaviour, however trivial or important.

The Palace:
A Centre of Aristocratic Art and
Learning During the Baroque Era

Every age evolves its own characteristic forms to project its image and creates an architectural frame within which to display it. The Mediterranean world of antiquity expressed itself politically and culturally in festive or stately processions, fine oratory and spectacles. Shows were much loved, some sporting, some sensational, others, such as the gladiatorial combats and the fights between men and beasts, even sadistic. Miniature sea battles for which whole arenas were filled with water were enacted. Life and politics in southern Europe then, as now, were carried on publicly with rhetoric. The outer shells of these spectacles remain as crumbling ruins: in Rome, for example, the Forum, the arches of Titus, Trojan and Constantine, the Colosseum and the theatre of Marcellus.

The spirit of the early Middle Ages that arose with the Holy Roman Empire is embodied, as far as the ruling classes were concerned, in the glittering chain of imperial palaces (Kaiserpfalzen) and castles (Reichsburgen). The extensive monastic buildings of that time still bear witness to monasticism as a spiritual movement charged with the preservation and transmission of learning. The high Middle Ages have left as architectural testimony to their attitude to life and view of the universe, in which their worldliness and spirituality were so curiously interwoven, the great Gothic cathedrals. Symbols of the new Jerusalem and 'citadels of God', they soared upwards, dominating the town. They were the scene of all social and artistic activities: ceremonial masses on the high days of the Church, religious plays and, outside the church porch, jurisdiction and political announcements.

The aristocratic culture of the Renaissance was polarized between urban palace and country house. Town and country were contrasting worlds, each with its own literary and artistic repertory of theatre, music, poetry, painting and architecture. In the baroque however, all these elements came together as the palace developed into an enclosed and complete work of art in itself that entirely fulfilled any yearning for artistic expression and display that might be felt by an aristocracy under the sway of an absolute ruler. With its great hall, state staircase, galleries, drawing-rooms and ballrooms, its chapel, music room, theatre, collections of art and curios, cabinets of porcelain and mirrors, orangery, magnificent stables and coach-houses, it united all courtly functions under one roof.

The most brilliant form of self-display in the aristocratic society of the baroque courts were the festivals, brilliant entertainments not without a political motive. In these festivities the attitudes and cultural assumptions of the absolutist era found their true and vital expression. After months of complicated and detailed preparation they could often last for weeks together. Practically all the members of court society were actors in a play that ran from dawn to dusk, players cast in permanent, profusely interrelated and symbolic roles. Like the complex structure of the baroque churches, the palace appeared in the consciousness of the period as a highly concentrated, permanent *theatrum mundi*, a world theatre.

The Rites of Reception

What scenes and interludes, speeches and gestures constituted that world theatre set amid the painted scenery of baroque palaces and parks? Let us begin at the beginning with the ceremonies that accompanied the arrival and reception of guests. Even this curtain-raiser was most subtly varied and modulated according to the importance, rank, merit and character of the visitor from the outer world. The first majestic scene through which the newcomer was ushered into the enchanted realm of the palace was the court of honour, varying in size according to the dimensions of the main mansion.

10

This significant introductory area, midway between open air and formal architecture, could be compared to an overture in music, giving a taste of things to come. The guest, having been driven over one of the immensely long converging drives that radiated across the extensive parkland, was finally conducted through the narrowing transformation scene of garden architecture towards the central point of the axis, to draw up in the palace forecourt, a horseshoe-shaped area half-ringed with splendid frontages. He alights from the carriage. Lackeys hurry forward to brush the dust from his hat, coat and shoes, for in the days before metalled roads even a short journey could leave the traveller looking like a baker. If his guest is of high and equal rank, the master of the house will receive him on the palace threshold. Trustworthy contemporary descriptions of the customs attending the arrival of guests, a ritual comparable only to those of the Byzantine court, enable us even today to relive at secondhand every stage of the ceremony.

As soon as His Majesty, the King of Prussia, was informed of his distinguished guests' approach, he came himself a quarter mile to greet them, accompanied by their Royal Highnesses, his three brothers, and after welcoming them, turned back to the palace. The King of Denmark and the King of Poland, however, continued their entry into Potsdam in the following order:

The Corps of Postillions, fifty in number, were in the lead, and sounded their posthorns. Next came a great many huntsmen proceeded by a head forester. There followed a company of the guard, some leading horses belonging to the king and margraves, and after them the gentlemen-in-waiting and high court officials headed by the Lord Chief Marshal. Behind these were the three margraves, directly followed by a sumptuous eight-horse, royal Prussian coach in which His Majesty, the King of Denmark, sat on the right and His Majesty, the King of Poland on the left. The rear of the procession was brought up by the Lifeguards, sounding their trumpets and drums.

Ranged on the right of the inner courtyard were the Lifeguards and the Swiss, on the left a battalion of Grenadiers; outside the palace yard, however, stood the well-armed yeoman militia men who fired three volleys as the procession passed through, whereupon thirty-six demi-cannon stationed in the park replied with three more shots.

His Majesty received his high-born visitors at the foot of the palace staircase and, after he had embraced them and accompanied them to their magnificent apartments, conversed with them in his cabinet for a long time.

The correlation between social and architectural order in the palace building is most clearly reflected in the role assigned to the main staircase in the subtly graded protocol. That important architectural element was the ideal device for indicating hair-fine degrees of social rank. In the baroque theatre of ceremony the grading of the subject's position was exactly defined by the number of steps his overlord descended in order to greet him. The manner in which the host received his guest at the top of the stairway, halfway down or even at its foot, measured the social distance between the two and put the latter very firmly in his place.

The entrance hall and main staircase were situated in the architectural centre of the palace, the line of their ascent clearly traceable on the exterior frontage. Their main function was clearly not communication between separate storeys and the different offices performed by the various departments, such as cellars, kitchens and dining-room. They were to a far greater extent an extravagantly decorated framework for the reception ceremony. In Germany especially this ritual use resulted in some of the most splendid staircases in the whole of western post-classical architecture.

1 *Turin, Palazzina di Stupinigi (1729–1736): Central view of the palace designed for Vittorio Amadeo II of Piedmont by Filippo Juvara as a hunting headquarters, a purpose emphasized by the statue of a stag on the dome of the dominating central portion. The building is far larger than a mere hunting lodge and is distinguished by its remarkable shape. Two diagonal axes cross in the lofty central building, forming four long, low wings. This star-shaped ground plan was an Italian peculiarity that never spread to France or the Germanic countries. Architects such as Fischer von Erlach used it only in imaginary projects, although it is a form particularly suited to palaces surrounded by gardens.*

2 *Rome, Villa Madama: The Roman town residence of Cardinal Giulio de Medici, later Pope Clement VII, was begun in 1517 after a design by Raphael. The uncompleted building was badly damaged during the sack of Rome (a month of looting by the army of Emperor Charles V in 1527), after which Antonio da Sangallo continued the work but did not finish. Later the house came into the possession of a natural daughter of Charles V, 'Madama' Margherita di Parma, after whom it was named. The frontage is typical of the Roman High Renaissance. Its individual appeal comes from the facade's mixture of brick and hewn stone, and from the regular placing of the windows, relieved by a rhythmic alternation of pediments. Horizontal bands and vertical window frames balance and harmonize the proportions of height and width. Apart from the building's interest as an example of a Roman palace and of Raphael's architectural design, it is remarkable for its ornaments and the 'grotesque' decorations by Giovanni da Udine, based directly on the ancient Roman finds discovered at that time.*

Frequently these stair wells occupy what seems to modern eyes an altogether disproportionate part of the palace's total volume, more even than the principal audience chamber or other rooms of state. Different indeed from the priorities of modern house design; the nearest though still distant approach being the stairways in public institutions or the mansions of Victorian magnates. In the state staircase of the baroque age architecture, sculpture, furnishings and illusional painting strive together like friendly rivals, each enhancing the other to achieve a glorious consummation. Among the most distinguished examples are those in the palaces of Pommersfelden and in Brühl, the residence of the Elector of Cologne. The sumptuous architecture of the latter, significantly enough, serves to this day as a fit setting for ceremonial state receptions in the otherwise rather austerely-minded German Federal Republic. Supreme among baroque staircases of state, however, is that of the Würzburg *Residenz*, unforgettable for its festive, almost musical, three-dimensional composition overarched by a magnificent ceiling painted by the leading decorator of the day, Giovanni Battista Tiepolo.

The role of the staircase as a stage for the play of courtly life fills many pages in the books of court etiquette handed down to us. Thus in 1690, during the election of Josef I in Augsburg, when the Elector of Mayence paid his official visit to the king he was received 'at the foot of the stairs' by the Lord Chamberlain and Chief Steward and conducted 'up two flights' to where the future emperor awaited him. When the Archbishop of Treves took leave of the King of Bohemia at the end of his official visit 'His Royal Majesty accompanied him to the head of the stairs, in spite of his protests and entreaties, so that his Majesty could watch until the Elector Archbishop was out of sight'. This lingering 'seeing off' was considered a special mark of favour and courtesy and as such was particularly noted by contemporary reporters.

In the *Ceremoniale Palatinatum* of 1700 an extraordinary amount of detailed attention is paid to the significance of the graduated reception and leavetaking ceremonies. The King of Bohemia and Hungary, for instance, stood at the top of the stairs to receive a Prince Elector, thus did not come down to meet him. When a return visit was paid, however, the Elector and his courtiers waited halfway down the staircase. While one set of rules existed to order the arrivals and departures of princes according to their respective ranks, another was dedicated to the reception of ambassadors from foreign powers. We know from Lünig's 'Book of Ceremony' that, in accordance with the rating of the power they represented, ambassadors were expected to maintain not only a proportionate wealth of servants, horses, carriages and costly furniture, but also 'wide and well-lit stairs'. It was customary for the ambassador to come down as far as the top of the last two steps to greet the king's deputed chamberlain. If the messenger came from a lesser power, a princedom for example, the ambassador would remain higher up the staircase, three or four steps below the first landing, perhaps, depending on the importance of the visitor.

The rules of the intricate game of court etiquette, especially those relating to the great staircase, illustrate how integral a part the architectural form of the baroque palace played in framing and ordering the lives of its inhabitants.

Gallery and Chapel

A subordinate but still highly ceremonial area, indispensable to the proper reception of visitors, was the gallery through which the royal host would personally conduct any particularly distinguished guests. To describe the gallery as an overgrown corridor set with doors to the various rooms that led off it would be greatly to underrate its functions. It had a far more comprehensive and symbolic importance. In addition to its use in the reception of distinguished guests, the gallery played a regular part in the ruler's ritualized daily routine. His day began with the apparently ordinary and everyday human activity of getting up, which in royal circles had to be conducted with strict ceremony and allegorical overtones to veil its banality. At the court of Louis XIV, who encouraged his deification as *Roi Soleil* and the 'New Apollo', the rising of the king from his bed was compared with the rising of the sun or *leveé du soleil*, whence it became known as the *leveé*. During this ceremony high-ranking nobles considered it an honour to perform tasks that would normally have been left to servants. One handed the king his shirt, another held the crystal bowl of scented water so that he could give his face and hands the proverbial 17th-century 'cat lick'. Still another helped him into his complicated succession of clothes and state robes, as differentiated as the court ceremonial itself, to which the artificiality of the huge wig and high-heeled shoes bore eloquent witness.

As soon as the ordinary mortal had been transfigured into a king, it was time for morning prayer in the palace chapel. *Louis Quattorze* had seen to it that this too should be a fit setting for the Sun King and heighten the prestige of his royal person, as is well illustrated by one detail from this religious spectacle. During mass only the king might look at the altar, on a level with God so to speak, or only very little lower, whereas those of the court who were present had to fix their eyes on the king. Here the role of courtiers as stage extras waiting on the performance of the king is made very clear.

In the next act the high nobility played slightly larger, even speaking, parts. After the service the King of France paced through his seventy-three meter gallery. In the gallery at Versailles the wall opposite the windows was panelled down its whole length with huge expanses of looking-glass, an enormously expensive undertaking at that time, and one that could have been carried out only by the king's appointed glass manufacturers. On the one hand these mirrors reflected and intensified the light from the real windows in the manner of a theatrical illusion, extending the space into infinity. On the other hand, they afforded the monarch the narcissistic pleasure of admiring his person in a long, if broken, series of reflections as he made his stately progress down the hall. Moreover, the cunning arrangement of looking-glasses threw back multiple images of the bowing courtiers ranged along either side of the gallery, reflecting the submissive delight of the individuals picked out to receive a few gracious words from their sovereign, and the deep despair of those who were ignored.

In addition to its several social and ceremonial functions, the Hall of Mirrors has a distinct symbolic content. At either end lies a room filled with allegorical paintings, one group representing the destruction wrought by war, the other the creative power of peace. Between these two opposite poles stretches the length of the gallery. The vaulted ceiling is adorned with huge paintings of the battles fought (and of course won) by Louis XIV. Inset between these colourful, chronologically ordered records of the king as warlord are others depicting his life as a wise ruler and prince of peace and showing the benevolence with which the political power of the French king was wielded.

Baroque galleries—anticipating the modern concept of an art gallery—harbour other adornments and functions. In place of the mirrored images of the royal household, there might be portraits, pictures, or even painted representations of the heavy wall-hangings beloved of the baroque period. These paintings by ever more important, or at any rate fashionable and expensive, masters testified to the artistic taste and financial resources of the

14

3

3   Rome, Palazzo Barberii: the back of the palace, seen from the garden. The building, begun by Carlo Maderno and Borromini in 1625 and completed by Bernini in 1633, was the town residence of Pope Urban VIII a member of the Roman family Barberini. The momumental quality of this masterpiece of the high baroque, produced by the best Roman architects of the period, still recalls the palaces of the 16th century. In plan and style it resembles Baldassare Peruzzi's Villa Farnesina built at the beginning of the century. The order of columns in the garden facade is derived from principles applied in ancient Rome and treated as architectural law during the Renaissance. Here it is seen at its most exact: Doric columns on the ground floor, Ionic on the first floor, Corinthian at the top. Its direct model may have been the nearby Colosseum, in which the same combination of arched colonnade and half-columns in series can be found.

collector. In the palace of Sanssouci at Potsdamm, for example, when Frederick the Great was prevented by bad weather from walking in the park with his favourite whippets, he took his exercise dryfoot in the picture gallery, passing in front of his treasured Old and New Masters, as if they were his 'tall fellows' of the grenadiers on parade. He marched down the line, pausing now and again to study a detail, just as he might have stopped to inspect more closely some item of a soldier's uniform.

As undeviating as the gallery is the long perspective of state rooms, the suite so typical of the baroque palace. Room opens out of room, a sumptuous perspective of double doors carrying the glance to a distant focal point. To hold the eye, that point was usually marked by some striking item of decoration: a giant Chinese vase of great value, a classical statue in a niche, a handsome piece of furniture or an eye-deceiving fresco, difficult to distinguish from reality at that distance, giving the impression that the perspective continued even further into an infinite suite of rooms or into far-reaching pleasure gardens. It was the Italians who first used the *trompe d'oeil* in their late renaissance villas and palazzi. Being so perfectly attuned to the taste for theatrical effect and general illusion, it was eagerly adopted into the palace architecture of the baroque period in lands north of the Alps.

The suite is an expression of the dominating theme of baroque palace design: rectilinear arms stretching out from the main axis of the building in an endless succession of magnificent rooms. Drawing the eye upwards and onwards, its form and content follow the same basic organisational idea as the whole baroque mansion and, still more, the baroque garden.

The long suites of state apartments are now museum pieces, mere empty shells of their former selves. That they were once filled with life and movement we know from contemporary accounts by the people who took part. For liveliness, exact observation, wit and narrative skill few can compare with those of Liselotte von der Pfalz, a German princess transplanted to France, who strikes today's reader as an accurate and reliable reporter. Her letters are of the greatest interest to social historians, and still make delicious reading. We have her to thank for the best record of court life at Versailles.

One of her innumerable letters, dated the 14th of December, 1676, describes a typical day at the French court.

'... first to Versailles, where we were busy the whole day through, for from morning till three o'clock we went hunting, and when we came back from hunting we changed our clothes and went up to play cards. There we stayed till seven in the evening; from thence we passed on to the play, which did not finish until half past ten, after which we had supper and then went to the ball, which lasted till three in the morning, and so to bed. ....'

The High Table

A high point in the daily routine was the royal dinner, which was also ritualised in fine detail and taken in public. Seated at a raised table, the cynosure of all eyes, the king ate alone, surrounded by a special staff of approved tasters and servers, as well as a Master of Ceremonies who accompanied the simple processes of eating and drinking with ecstatic cries of 'The King eats!', 'The King drinks!'. Other officials loudly announced the names of the separate courses. Here too, as at the royal leveé, the highest nobles were privileged to act as servants, waiting on the sovereign personally and proffering him the dishes sent in from the kitchen. An important member of the cast at this august and formal meal was of course the king's personal physician, who would from time to time counsel the sovereign behind the back of his hand not to partake of one dish or another. It was not too great an abstinence for the king to send one glazed boar's head back to the kitchen untasted when there were twenty-four other courses to choose from. The refusal was far from unwelcome to the head cook, who made a lucrative business of selling the food left over from the royal table, a perquisite much envied by less fortunate officials.

It was not only at Versailles that the monarch's meals proceeded with such pomp. Even the comparatively modest court of the King of Prussia in Potsdam, on the occasion of the state visit of the Kings of Denmark and Saxony in 1709, staged a number of banquets commensurate with the rank and importance of the royal guests, which Christian Heinrich Gutthern describes for us in his *Life and Acts of Frederick I*. In connection with these ceremonial dinners an almost insoluble problem of etiquette arose: how could two equal-ranking kings both sit in the place of honour at their royal host's right hand? The Prussian Master of Ceremonies must have been a veritable Solomon of etiquette. It was decided that the two Majesties should sit there on alternate days, the choice of position on the first day being decided by lot.

Once the difficult questions of seating protocol had been settled, the leading nobles were richly compensated, not only by the quality of the food, but also by 'two choirs of trumpets and drums' sounded at table. The acoustic climax of this musical feast was reached when the king and queen drank. On these occasions the French horns were drowned by the firing of six demi-cannon (heavy guns) whereas, when lesser royalties such as the margraves and their wives quenched their thirst they had to make do with only three eight-pounders.

Festivities at Court

A state banquet was the central point of courtly festivals, which were also ritualised to the highest degree and conducted according to the strictest etiquette.

To describe these festivities as grand parties to amuse and relax the courtiers after their strenuous days would be to do them less than justice. Their purpose was rather to exalt still further the image of state, sovereign and court. Pretexts for highly organized state occasions of that kind were provided by coronations or—in the Holy Roman Empire—an imperial election, the birth of an heir, a christening or, in more austere vein, a royal funeral. The main objective of the enormous pomp and intricate ceremonial arrangements was to demonstrate the power and glory of the state, and not, as often supposed today, merely to satisfy the personal desire of the ruler and his minions for amusement and display. The court poet Besser graphically formulates that duty to represent the state, duty being the operative word: 'Magnificence is necessary to a prince, for he is God's deputy; God shows his magnificence in his outward works; as God in his creation, so must the prince be radiant and shine in all his outward works'. Here in a nutshell is the social and moral justification and the declared policy of the baroque court in all its megalomaniac extravagance. The philosophic concept of the prince as God's representative on earth ennobles his position as ruler, military commander, peaceful administrator commissioner of works of art, patron of all art and learning and—what must be our chief concern here—as builder. Godlike, in the role of a secular demiurge, he operates as a lordly creator, conjuring up a new world on this earth, a paradigm of the divine Genesis. Elevated by this symbolic comparison with the Supreme Being, the mortal prince withdraws from all petty critical assessment of his image as manysided overlord of the arts. Criticism of a ruler by the Grace of God quickly becomes blasphemy to be discredited and punished as such.

It is now clear why the gardens of Versailles had to be started literally 'from the ground up'. The earth, too, at the beginning of Genesis was 'without form and void'. It was the very chaos and bleakness of the original site that gave the establishment of the *château* and gardens its creative quality. In the same way, the 'shining radiance' of the king expressed itself in the creation and organization of the complicated festivals of state for which the palace and park served as earthly paradise, Garden of Eden and a setting for quasi-religious rites.

The festivals were in the nature of theatrical productions and as such were immortalized in large, richly illustrated folio volumes. It is from these works that our knowledge of the court festivals is derived and when we, who live in such an utterly different social and cultural environment, leaf through those pages of detailed description and fine copper engravings the past delights are brought back to us, real and comprehensible.

The full range of the baroque festival cannot be grasped if we imagine, as we tend to do today, that it was mainly a matter of dancing by candlelight, beautifully dressed, in a lavishly decorated ballroom. The fête of the baroque period was always a whole succession of entertainments. Like the architecture, it spread its net well beyond the palace walls into the surrounding drives and gardens. Thus there were festive processions to be judged by their length and the numbers of floats and participators, like the Lord Mayor's Show or the Battle of Flowers at Nice. In the late seventeenth century they consisted of fancy-dress parades, usually held in some central area of the park. They were not without precedent. Quite early in the Italian renaissance aristocratic society had displayed itself in similarly grandiose pageants. The name 'triumphs' (*trionfi*) given to the decorated waggons that took part betrays their inspiration in the ancient triumphal processions of victorious Roman generals. Certain set pieces of scenery were considered appropriate to that tradition, especially features of ancient classical architecture, such as gateways, arches, obelisks, statues, pillars and pyramids. In spite of their ephemeral nature (they were usually constructed of *papier maché*, or of canvas stretched on a wooden framework, and supplemented with live plants and flowers), they were valued as true works of art and were designed and made by the most admired artists of the day. We know that Leonardo, Michelangelo, Bramante, Peruzzi and Raphael were among those who supervised the scenic architecture of renaissance masques. In the baroque age the same tradition of festival design was carried on by artists of the rank of Bernini, Rubens, Mansart, Fischer von Erlach and Lukas von Hildebrandt.

The renaissance ruler, like his baroque successor, concerned himself personally with the planning, arrangement, content and appearance of these pageants. He it was who conceived the original idea. It was the task of the Court Poet as deviser of entertainments to expand the royal brainwave into 'inventions' in other words to put it into presentable literary form. Such entertainments, moreover, were not to fall below the ceremonial standards expected in the royal pageant, theatre or banqueting hall. That was the responsibility of the Lord Chamberlain as chief Master of Ceremonies.

Characteristic of the spirit of the age was the preference for mythological allegory in these entertainments. All Olympus was drawn into the service of the baroque masque, from Zeus, Mars and Apollo to Athene, Hera and Diana. It is not without a certain irony that it was the more dissolute among the princes, such as Augustus the Strong of Saxony, who best appreciated the

4 *Tivoli near Rome, the Villa d'Este: a partial view of the so-called Fontana dell'Organo Idraulicok, a water organ. The villa, begun by Pirro Ligorio in 1550 for Cardinal Ippolito II d'Este, the nephew of a pope, is world-famous for its amazing terraced gardens. Ingeniously the steeply sloping terrain has been used to create an unforgettable composition of architecture, vegetation, fountains and cascades, anticipating the use of water in the later French baroque gardens. The water organ is a technical marvel by the Frenchman Claude Venard, drawing the power for its rhythmically musical water-spouts from the natural flow of the Aniene river, which supplies the water for the whole garden, with its 500 cascades. Statues of Orpheus and Apollo, both mythical personifications of music were chosen to adorn the water organ. Perhaps Orpheus, who drew his lost wife to the gates of the underwold with the playing of his lyre, also refers to the shadowy cult of grottos, so loved in the gardens of the renaissance and baroque periods.*

4

5 *Tivoli near Rome, Villa d'Este: view of one of the terraced waterfalls. The vista of terraces, and jetting or falling waters in an architectural setting embellished with greenery gives the impression of some magnificent stage scene. The crowning eagle was added as a heraldic emblem of the Austrian empire.*

appearance on festive occasions of the purest and most virginal figure of ancient myth, the chaste Diana, whose ever unsuccessful suitors met with such distressing metamorphoses, being turned, as often as not, into stags torn to pieces by hounds. It was the same Augustus the Strong, King of Poland and Elector of Saxony, still remembered as the prototype of the baroque prince *par excellence* for his artistic perception and love of display, who was unrivalled as an inventive impresario of grandiose festivities. His numerous castles and palaces in and around Dresden provided a continual change of scene. Here again contemporary chroniclers provide us in the orotund style of the period with lavish descriptions of one of his most famous feasts, on this occasion to celebrate the wedding of his son and heir to an imperial princess in 1719. In the spirit of the love of mythological subjects, the masque performed at the Dutch Palace on the 10th of September was called *The Diversion of the Planets*. Each planet appeared in person to invite the wedding guests to a special feast in their honour. The ensuing planetary diversions were staged in different places. We will examine more closely the 'Festival of the Four Elements' which was under the protection of Jupiter.

The arena in which this mythologically inspired work of art was played was the ideal setting for such a spectacle: the palatial Zwinger orangery in Dresden. The entertainment was a masque on horseback, a late, courtly descendant of the medieval tourney. Dressed in fantastic costumes, each symbolic of one of the four elements, the horsemen were divided into the four quadrilles representing earth, air, fire and water respectively. First came some attractive figure riding, then the so-called *Carrousel* and Horse Ballet. The last item was inspired by Vienna. In 1667, to celebrate an imperial wedding, a Horse Ballet was performed at the castle there. So great was its success that, like the Vienna Boys' Choir, the institution still survives as a first-class proprietary article and relic of the old imperial splendour, we know it as the Spanish Riding School in Vienna.

At the main gates of the Zwinger a special attraction was erected, a pleasingly composed contraption known as the 'Chaos Machine'. It housed an assortment of the mechanical toys and theatrical machines considered indispensable to the baroque stage or festival. The Chaos Machine displayed the Four Elements in constant movement, and at their centre sat an effigy of Jupiter, the provider of the feast.

The cavaliers appeared in a colourful train, each troop flanked by a mounted band of musicians. The first quadrille was 'Fire', the riders all decked in red and gold, helmets flowing with flaming scarlet ostrich plumes. At their head rode Augustus, King of Poland and Elector of Saxony, in person. The second quadrille, 'Water', was led by the Elector's heir. He and his followers were clad in pale blue and silver and wore dolphinesque helmets. Next came th 'Earth' quadrille costumed in dark brown and gold, with the Duke of Weissenfels in front. The last quadrille represented 'Air' and was headed by the Duke of Wurtemberg. The costumes were mainly white with a wing motif to symbolize the light and airy element.

The quadrille riders staged mock fights or jousts and tilting at the rings, sports derived from the medieval tournament. For the latter exercise sixteen pyramids were erected in the main square of the palace with rings suspended between them.

A gallant spectacle that had never been included in the old tourneys, however, was the 'Ladies' Carrousel', a race for the gentler sex. The leading ladies, fashionable members of the Augustan court, dressed in dashing mythological disguises, each sat in a light racing carriage driven by a sporting cavalier. The place of honour, of course, was reserved for the King-Elector's *maîtresse en titre*, who at that time was the enchanting Countess Cosell, the 'secret' Queen of Saxony, as witty as she was beautiful. Her driver was the King of Denmark, the outrider no less a person than Augustus himself.

It was taken for granted in those days that the King's family should be among the audience. However much they might gnash their teeth in private, in public they had to witness the homage paid to the royal mistress with the dignity, decorum and reserve expected in such situations according to the universal code of court etiquette.

The power of a baroque-age ruler to harness the resources of the whole countryside to his will in order to carry out some entertainment, festival or amusement he had planned was almost unlimited. A characteristic instance occurred in the winter of 1728 at the Court of Augustus the Strong. A magnificent sledging picnic on ice had long been in preparation. ... When there was an overnight thaw that would have sent all the sledges to the bottom. Without delay 300 peasants were drummed up to carry thousands of cartloads of snow from the upper slopes and tip them on to the mushy picnic-route.

One aspect, already touched on in connection with the Ladies' Carrousel, namely the almost socially accepted, highly formal relationship with the 'official' mistresses (the monarch simply had to have one, even if he did not care for women, or preferred monogamy on moral grounds), is illustrated by a lively letter from the Baron Pollnitz at the Saxon court.

Even the wooing of the lady in question was a welcome excuse for a mythological, allegorical masquerade and prelude for the theatre-obsessed prince. For him every event was transformed into a drama to be acted out in front of an audience. On the other hand, he made no move without being sure of a numerous and well informed public. The royal household had to alternate rapidly between the roles of observer and actor.

Augustus the Strong is once again the hero of the story. After a long 'siege' he had succeeded in breaking through the defences of the fascinating Aurora von Königsmark. At last she had given in to his persuasion and consented to become his official mistress. A fitting reception had now to be prepared for her and her sister. The Moritzburg, a hermitage in the woods, was chosen as the site for the occasion. The two ladies—in spite of the amorous reason for the party—were dressed as warlike amazons. They were driven into the wood in a splendid carriage and suddenly found themselves before the gates of a beautiful palace. The coachman reined in his horses, the gates opened wide, and out stepped Diana with her train of pretty nymphs. The goddess addressed the noble young lady of Königsmark in well composed rhymed couplets, punning on her classical name of 'Aurora', and invited her into the palace, where the forest deities would pay homage to her. The young women were ushered into a festal hall decorated with subjects from myths of Diana, with allusions to the goddess's solitary woodland life, her realm and her hunting, including the punishment of the prying Actaeon and the death of Endymion. Then a table laden with food and drink rose through the floor, propelled by machinery—a favourite trick at baroque banquets. While they ate a little orchestra of arcadian 'rustics' played sweet music on flutes, pipes and shawms.

Only the promised woodland deities were still missing. Who was the instigator of all this is not hard to guess. And sure enough, when the demigods at last appeared, they were led by the royal lover himself, disguised as Pan. His courtiers were dressed as subordinate forest godlings of antiquity.

'Diana' seated 'Pan' at the side of his Aurora, and the feast proceeded to the accompaniment of polished gallantries, an exchange of remarks and replies stiff with literary references in the fashionably coquettish, allusive tone of the period, and all according to an established etiquette.

Pages 24–25:
6 *Fontainebleau by the Seine: a general view of the palace and park of what was the traditional hunting lodge of the kings of France from Louis VII (1137–1180) onwards. expanded to its present form by François I (1515–1547). Surrounded by the wide horizons of the Seine valley, the extensive palace and grounds are typical of the French renaissance* châteaux, *elsewhere to be seen in their full glory only in the region of the Loire. The present complex building developed from the mantling of the medieval core and repeated extensions carried out in later periods. The renaissance garden with its spreading lawns is situated on one side of the palace and not arranged in axial relationship to the main building as in French baroque gardens such as Versailles. It still suggests a free, unmanipulated use of land. As a* 'hortus conclusus', *an entity in its own right, the renaissance garden was not a formal extension of the palace ground-plan into the open, but remained an added amenity.*

7   *Fontainebleau: the 'wing of the beautiful chimneys', which takes its name from the design of the roof with its variously shaped chimney stacks. The plan and decoration of this section date back to the Italian architects imported by François I, the most prominent of whom, Rosso Fiorentino and Primaticcio, gave the building its individual character. Whereas the external Italian features have largely been overlaid by the classic French palace style (one has only to compare the typical French roof with its contemporary Italian counterpart), the temperament and idiom of the two representatives of Italian Mannerism live on in the paintings and decoration of the interior. This elegant, courtly mixture of the French and Italian styles has been dubbed 'School of Fontainebleau' and is France's most original and individual contribution to international Mannerism.*

26

9

8 *Fontainebleau: view across the carp pond to the 'chimney wing' and Francis I's terrace. Not visible in the picture is the 'apartement de la reine' an annexe to the chimney wing on the opposite side. During the earlier days of absolutism, that is to say up to the reign of Louis XIV, when the court finally moved to Versailles, the Château of the Carp Pond, as Fontainebleau was sometimes called, was the brilliant and uncontested centre of French baroque culture, as well as being the royal country seat as distinct from the King's town residence, the Louvre in Paris.*

9 *Fontainebleau; the carp pond. In the middle of the tree-girt pond is a little island pavilion. Guests at court parties were ferried there in boats to admire the view of the palace reflected in the water. The pavilion now standing on the islet is a 19th century reconstruction of the original.*

When the meal was finished a stag was let loose and there was a *battue*, for they were after all in the realm of the huntress deity, Diana.

After that there was a complete change of scene, there being nothing that bored the baroque audience more than long waits and repetition. Now a forest lake was revealed, by its banks a sumptuous tent in the Turkish style. There had been some sharp political encounters with the Ottoman Empire of late, and the scene was no doubt a significant reference to the oriental way of life, with its seraglios, harems, harem guards, eunuchs, abductions and a sophisticated erotic literature specialising in amorous refinements.

After the fatiguing diversion of chasing the stag, refreshments were served in silver baskets by twenty-four handsome young Turks in costly eastern attire. To remain consistent with the oriental theme, a whole Turkish royal household was produced, centred naturally on the royal lover himself. That is to say that from a second splendid tent there suddenly appeared high officials of the harem, played by courtiers and followed by the suite of the King Elector, who had meanwhile changed his garb into that of the Great Sultan. (One really wonders how members of this aristocratic, 17th century society,

29

constantly occupied with dressing and undressing, putting costumes and wigs on and taking them off, changing their disguises as if they were strolling players, ever had time to do anything more important.)

The Great Sultan Augustus laid down beside his adored Aurora on a sofa to watch a dance entertainment in eastern style.

After that came a tour of the lake, and then the performance of the obligatory play. When supper was over the ball began.

At a suitable moment the high-born lovers retired to consummate the 'left-hand' nuptials so officially celebrated and established. According to the manners of the age, the Queen, for all her imperial Hapsburg blood, could do nothing to prevent these improper goings-on. With the inherited obtuseness of her nature, it probably never occurred to her to attempt to.

Allegorical costumes, formal ballets and masques were not confined to the celebrations of great events. A succession of smaller functions of the same kind went on all through the year and needed no special excuse.

The almost obligatory wearing of fancy dress as an ingredient of every party was taken for granted at the baroque court, where a theatrical elite set the tone. Dancing or balls took place practically every evening after dinner, and often lasted into the small hours. The masked balls, made up of music, costume, dancing and ballet on the model of the Italian *redotto* were an indispensable part of court life. Special, splendidly decorated ballrooms were built to serve as a fitting background for these entertainments. Even distinguished elder statesmen were obliged to wear fancy dress if they wanted to remain at the ball for political reasons, and reluctantly donned the mask and costume of Harlequin, Pan or some other disguise.

The larger courts maintained their own permanent companies of actors and dancers, whose duty it was to give regular productions. Touring performers visited the smaller courts at frequent intervals. At these lesser residences the courtiers themselves were expected to be able to perform a masque.

The summit of all these entertainments, in which acting, music, dance, illusional painting, sham architecture, lighting effects, mechanical devices and poetry combined to create a complete and brilliant work of art, was the baroque opera. To provide premises worthy of this art form, minor princes such as the Margraves of Bayreuth-Ansbach, crippled themselves financially for decades, an enterprise our contemporaries, who can watch opera for a comparatively trifling sum, can only admire with amazement and without reserve. It is thanks to those princely patrons that we have today the early 18th-century Bayreuth Opera House, one of the most exquisite theatrical buildings of that epoch, in which we can still feel the authentic spirit and atmosphere of the baroque musical theatre.

As well as the highly stylized entertainments held inside the palace and its grounds, there were country excursions and picnics which the courtiers also managed to turn into play-acting. These much-loved expeditions were staged in the arcadian sheep-farming style so popular in the literature of the time. The light-hearted participants went dressed in idealized rustic guise as farmers, countrymen, shepherds, gardeners or fishermen. They fancied themselves as the simple and happy country folk of idyllic poetry. Other sources were ancient legends of herdsmen such as Anacreon and Theocrites; Horace and Virgil were drawn on too, and examples taken from the Renaissance copied. In such rural surroundings the courtiers sought rest and relaxation after their strenuous life at court, but even here etiquette could not be entirely avoided and the masquerading as nymphs, shepherdesses, *belles jardinières* and rustic coquettes was conducted according to exact rules and allegorical ceremony.

The extreme example of an architectural setting for this courtly 'counter-culture' still exists today in Marie Antoinette's little hamlet on the borders of the park of Versailles. In '*Le Hameau*', with its thatched farm resembling an over-sized doll's house, the ill-fated young Queen of France sought refuge from the formality of court life in the innocent occupations of the country, milking her well-groomed cows and making butter and cheese in her model dairy. A flock of pretty maids of honour in clogs, caps and aprons were there to help her. While occupied with their rustic tasks the charming dairymaids might occasionally glance over their shoulders at a courtier, also suitably clad in coarse peasant smock. Their discreetly boisterous advances, in tune with the setting, were coquettishly repelled, in imitation of the behaviour they had occasionally observed from afar, not without a shade of envy, in village or servant's hall. Fragonard, Watteau and Boucher, among others, have immortalised these scenes of artificial rusticity in paintings, drawings and engravings in which charm, artistic merit, fashionable mood and exact observation are salted with a certain ironical detachment from such frivolous nonsense.

The enthusiastic amateurs, of course, were never really in touch with the realities of the peasant world that inspired their arcadian amusements. In this matter as in others the court circles remained in a world of their own and avoided every unjustified familiarity that might have breached the barriers that protected the citadel of their aristocratic society. Nature, as they depicted it, remained unnatural, merely a charming game. Townspeople and peasants, for instance, were never invited to palace festivities unless it was in order to laugh at the old-fashioned clothes worn by the wives and daughters of minor officials, or to play pranks, which made the courtiers scream with laughter, on the farmers and their families. Indeed, the refined society of the day took particular pleasure in inviting the peasants to court with the declared purpose of making them drunk, so that it could make fun of their unpolished manners and stammering speech and at the same time increase its own self esteem as a superior caste. The fun could even be heightened by tricks in questionable taste. At the bidding of His Serene Highness hidden pipes would squirt cold water under the skirts of the farmers' daughters.

Beneath the bright surface of courtly manners and fastidiousness lay the unbroken tradition of coarse insensitivity characteristic of the medieval nobility in relation to their social inferiors. There still existed an acceptance of moral oppression such as the *Jus primae noctis* or *Droit du seigneur*, the overlord's right to sleep with the daughter of a lowly tenant on the night before her wedding. Although the right was nearly always commuted into a fee, it might still depend on the bride's attractions.

No wonder this society was utterly bewildered in 1789, when its frivolous world was so rudely shattered. Louis XVI, the last French king of the old regime, was an empty husk in comparison with his altogether vital and powerful ancestor, Louis XIV. Typically, on the day he was arrested in his workshop, among the watches that were his hobby, all he found to write in his meticulously pedantic diary was what he had eaten for dinner that day. His wife, Queen Marie Antoinette, equally ignorant of the real world, was supposed to have suggested that her subjects, crying out for bread, should eat cake.

The Park

Picnics, excursions and other pseudo-rustic amusements belonged to that aesthetic, highly organised sphere which held as significant a place in the artistic consciousness of the epoch as the architectural monument of the

10 *Fontainebleau; a section of the* cour du Cheval Blanc *(White Horse Court), that took its name from a copy of the marble equestrian statue of Marcus Aurelius on the Capitol in Rome. The copy, now no longer present, was commissioned by Catherine de Medici, the Italian queen of Henri II. Today the courtyard is commonly called 'La Cour des Adieux', because it was here that the banished Emperor Napoleon took leave of his Old Guard during his retreat to Elba. What gives the spacious courtyard its special character is the great double outdoor stairway leading from court level to residential storey. The final version of the staircase was designed by Jean du Cerceau in 1634.*

11 *Fontainebleau: the Golden Door leading into the wing built from the plans of Gilles le Breton in the 16th century. At that time it was used as the main entrance to the palace. The richness of the gilding after which it was named is in attractive contrast to the solidity and plainness of the untreated limestone façade.*

33

12 *Fontainebleau: all detail from the Galerie François I was begun in 1531 and completed in the 1540s. The gallery was the work of those most gifted Italian decorators, Rosso Fiorentino and Primaticcio. 210 feet long and 20 feet wide, it was one of the most important productions of French palace design since the Renaissance. The brilliant apogee and full stop of this architectural form was the Hall of Mirrors at Versailles, built over a 100 years later (plate 24). The main function of the gallery as a parade ground for courtiers is complemented by the scenes depicted on the walls, drawing close, if flattering, parallels with the life and person of the sovereign. The wall paintings here show the deeds of François I, with mythological allusions to his prowess. The initial F carved on the panelling denotes his ubiquitous presence in the paintings. Nearly 300 years later Napoleon caused his initial N to be displayed in the rooms furnished by him at Fontainebleau, meaning in that way to connect himself with the royal tradition.*

palace itself, namely the baroque palace garden. An entirely artificial creation, laid out in regular geometrical patterns, it was an integral part of the whole complex scheme of the palace. It obeyed the same rules of axiality, symmetry and zones of graded importance. The grounds were an extension and continuation of the mansion's architecture, forming an excellent stage and backcloth for court festivities, with formal hedges and borders for the wings. Only as much nature was admitted as would make a suitable setting for the fancies of the baroque age.

The park's position halfway between nature and architecture was epitomised in the garden theatre, where in the summer months the court was entertained with plays of arcadian rusticity.

On hot summer days the artificial canals, ponds, fountains and springs were the scene of water ballets and miniature naval battles with the spectators dressed in antique costume; at nights the waters reflected ornamental illuminations and fireworks.

There were mazes too, twisting walks between high hedges that, instead of leading to some new vista, narrowed down to a blind alley. An example of this garden contrivance was the labyrinth designed by Le Nôtre for the park of Versailles. Besides the psychological contrast between its bewildering succession of turnings and dead ends and the widening views into the distance typical of the rest of the garden, the maze was conceived as a parable. The two figures placed at the entrance personified its moral and allegorical meaning. On one side stands an angel unwinding a skein of thread (a reference to Ariadne's thread that rescued Theseus from the minotaur's labyrinth); on the other the ancient fabulist Aesop with the skein rolled up. If the angel personifies the wisdom that can find its way unerringly through the maze of life, Aesop is a symbol of the maze's aesthetic and moral significance. For in his fables Aesop found a metaphorical yet playful method of pointing a human moral in animal guise. His talented imitator La Fontaine, who used the same allusive, hide-and-seek medium to mirror the foibles of his contemporaries, was greatly to the literary taste of the age.

This list by no means exhausts the attractions of the late seventeenth and early eighteenth century park. The baroque garden first reached its perfected form when Le Nôtre (sometimes spelt Le Nostre) designed the park at Versailles. With its ordered alternation of grass plot and grove, its canal stretching as far as the eye can see, it is the perfect example of a style that reigned supreme up to the late 18th century, when it was superseded by the 'English garden' a diametrically opposite type of park that has never dropped out of fashion.

Within its strictly geometrical framework, the baroque garden was full of treasures, variety and surprises. There were ornamental waters, watery 'tricks' and devices, outdoor playhouses, statues, groups of statues—indeed whole avenues of statues—and variegated paths as well as quantities of little gazebos and pavilions set among trees, flowering shrubs, lawns and hedges. From the wilderness the hand of man had created an 'earthly paradise', a dream of Arcadia where pain and death had no place, under a dome of sky set with sun, moon or stars.

Not least among the delights of the garden were the plants and flowers. The baroque princes were keen collectors and loved to assemble rare, exotic plants from every quarter of the globe to be lovingly planted, tended and multiplied in their domains. It was almost a mania. A fashionable addition to the park was an orangery, where orange and lemon trees from the shores of the Mediterranean could flourish in chilly northern climes. Soon special decorative building styles were invented to house the rare and fashionable fruit-trees. Why nothing was too good for them is understandable when we hear that 400 thalers, a small fortune in those days, was paid for one large, handsome orange tree. Other exotic species too were imported from the Mediterranean, Asia, Africa and America, and became high fashion. Many of them: laurels, pomegranates, pineapples, olive trees, myrtles, cedars, cypresses, American aloes and yews, became favourite emblems of the period. It was during the baroque age that the *Castanea equina*, better known to us as the horse chestnut tree, first arrived in Europe, where it was very soon domesticated. This wide variety of trees, shrubs, ornamental plants and flowers supplied a rich palette from which the expert gardeners could fashion their horticultural works of art. They hybridised, grafted, trellised and propped them up; with knife and shears they developed the craft of topiary. Bushes were moulded into geometrical, architectural shapes; in the world of the baroque palace, nothing could escape the passion for the formal. The balustrades along the terraces were enlivened by leafy pyramids, cubes, globes, even animal and human shapes in quite complex groups.

Embedded in this green universe were architectural miniatures in the taste of the period: so-called hermitages, tea pavilions, summerhouses, fantastic artificial ruins, monuments in memory of favourite dogs and horses and small versions of exotic buildings such as mosques and Moorish courtyards. In the park of Schwetzinger Palace a Mahommedan place of prayer was built for the imported Arab and Turkish workers on the estate. It could be said that in a baroque garden the whole historical and geographical contents of the world were represented on a diminished scale in architectural symbols.

Shielding the gardens from the crude outside world of nature were the stables, coach houses and other practical estate buildings. The upper classes were infected with horse mania and, as befitted the status of that noble animal, even such everyday structures as stables were designed—as they had been during the Renaissance too—in artistic form as veritable equine palaces. There were numerous costly equipages, ranging from the coronation coach, through various carriages of state, travelling carriages, smart pony-traps and hunting wagons to sledges. In both value and comfort they were in no way inferior to the modern luxury car. The name of a skilful coach-builder was whispered behind the hand on a level with that of the best cabinet-maker, portrait painter or silversmith.

Of great importance to the palace housekeeping, and not without the usual stately architectural adjuncts, were the pheasant preserves, which supplied the princely table with succulent game birds as a change from the homely farmyard fowl. Also highly prized for fine eating were peacocks, partridges and that new arrival from America, the turkey or *Galla indiana*, hence also known as 'the Indian fowl'.

Often very big aviaries, were constructed to house the collections of rare native and foreign birds that were the pride of ruling princes. Often they were extended into enclosures for other animals, not only quarry for the royal hunt or staged combats, such as stags, deer or bears, but also, still in accord with the contemporary passion for the exotic, rare beasts from overseas. One zoological garden that has continued its function uninterruptedly to the present day is in the grounds of Schönbrunn Palace.

A transitional zone, halfway between the purely architectural palace building and the outdoor but still architecturally conceived gardens, was the garden room or *sala terrena*. It was on ground level or half sunk below it, one or more of its sides opening on to the park. The decoration usually followed a theme, maybe an underwater cavern encrusted with shells, pillared with stalagmites and stalactites, adorned with model fish and other sea creatures and murmuring with cascades and fountains; a delicious refuge from the heat of summer.

36

13   Fontainebleau: the ballroom. This room too was the work of Rosso Fiorentino and Primaticcio. It was used for grand official occasions, balls, concerts and theatrical performances, the lustrous peak of an aristocratic civilization in the shadow of the crown. The room's dimensions (99 feet by 33 feet) are in accordance with the grandiose standards of their royal master.

The Courtly Hunt

The park finally merged into the private hunting grounds and open country, and with these we leave the palace premises to follow another important activity pertaining to the aristocratic way of life at a baroque court: the hunt.

Like the other courtly pastimes, it was more than a mere amusement or, in this case, an entertaining method of enriching the fare at court dinners with the spoils of the chase. Hunting, too, had evolved into something of a showpiece, a highly stylised ritual. Clothes for hunting were another excuse for disguises and fashionable extravagance, especially for the women. The obsession with mythological subjects could be given free rein. It was not considered at all odd for prince and courtiers to be dressed as an ancient god of the hunt with his train. His lady was only too pleased to appear as Diana followed by a bevy of nymphs.

The etiquette of the hunting field was laid down in precise detail and strictly enforced. The ceremonial laying out and display of the kill, testifying to the success of the principal huntsmen's efforts, was ritualized to the highest degree, and still survives in what they would have considered a degenerate form, when the day's bag is laid out at the end of a shoot. Such a display of royal skill was all part of the princely apothesis. But in this the baroque age was not alone. The ceremonial hunt has always been a privilege of the ruling caste, whether one thinks of the royal lion hunts in ancient Assyria, in which only the hand of the god-descended king was considered worthy of killing the king of beasts, or of the Egyptian hippopotamus hunts of the Pharaohs depicted on wall paintings and reliefs, or even of the hunting mania of the German princes in the early middle ages. Thus one of the chief reasons why Charlemagne, the founder of the first post-Roman empire on European soil, chose Aix-la-Chapelle for his chief residence was the proximity of rich hunting grounds in the depth of the trackless forests of the Ardennes. When other stations on the routes of the Holy Roman Emperor's perpetual progresses were developed as administrative centres, staging posts or palaces, their sites were partly determined with an eye to their hunting amenities. We have only to think of Hagenau in Alsace with its famous game reserves, or of the favourite hunting grounds of the Emperor Maximilian, 'the last knight of chivalry', in the Tyrol.

The hunt, regarded without question in the Middle Ages as a part of the lord's duties and rights, continued into the Renaissance as a lordly privilege, but by then was often distorted into grotesque exaggeration. Thus we know that at the relatively minor court of the Viscontis at Milan the boar-hunt had, for Prince Bernabó di Visconti, become one of the most important state activities, for which he kept a pack of 5,000 hounds to be fed by an aggrieved peasantry. The well being of that army of hungry quadrupeds directly affected the condition and lives of his human subjects. Anyone setting himself against this madness of hunting and hounds was liable to be cruelly punished. The perversion reached its apex in another scion of that extraordinary family, Giovanmaria di Visconti, who gained a grisly notoriety through his pack of hounds trained to hunt not animals but human beings.

Obviously in the etiquette-bound world of the 17th and 18th centuries the hunt was no longer marked by these perverse excesses, but it was still a ceremonial pageant demonstrating the power of the state. According to the carefully graduated court ritual, there was a pronounced differentiation of status between various types of hunt, hunting methods and, above all, the quarry chased.

Just as the open country had been transformed into the green architecture of a formal park, so the baroque huntsmen disdained the pursuit of sport in fields or woods left in a chaotic state of nature. Even their hunting grounds were stylized into a geometrical pattern expanded to megalomaniac proportions.

The most distinguished quarry, the red deer, was hunted on horseback. A pack of hounds routed the deer from covert and chased it until it was exhausted, followed by the mounted hunt. With his hunting knife the Master of Hounds (a position reserved for the prince) gave the *coup de grace*. This mixture of hunting and riding necessitated long avenues for the chase. The rides spread for miles through the forest, usually radiating from a centrally placed pavilion and joined at intervals by cross-paths, after the pattern of a spider's web. By means of this network of open rides the royal hunt could follow the trail to any part of the hunting grounds and cut off the animal's retreat.

In addition to this intricate system of communication the hunt-obsessed baroque princes built numbers of hunting lodges. Thus the Prince Elector Johann Wilhelm von der Pfalz—still affectionately remembered by the inhabitants of his former capital, Düsseldorf, as 'Jan Wellem'—had a hunting lodge built for himself in Bensberg by the Venetian 'architect knight' Count Matteo Alberti, which for size, splendour and artistic quality put some of the palaces of petty rulers in the shade.

Not seldom such lodges with their attached game preserves became the starting point and nucleus of subsequent palaces. The shining example is the founding of the late baroque Karlsruhe on the site of one of these hunting grounds. In 1715, the year in which his admired model, Louis XIV, died, the charismatic young Margrave Karl-Wilhelm von Baden-Durlach laid the foundation stone for a hunting-lodge the plans for which he had drawn with his own hand. From the circular central clearing where the ceremony took place 32 radiating rides starred out into the forest. The lodge was quite a modest building, partly in frame and plaster at first, but soon became a grand country mansion and later on the prince's chief palace at the heart of a new town extending into the forest. Here lived settlers from every land. Like true pioneers they had been attracted by tax exemptions, religious freedom and the prospect of full employment.

That this hunting mansion with its newly settled town should so quickly rival and finally supplant the old Durlach palace, the ancestral residence of the family throughout the Middle Ages and Renaissance, says much of the age's passion for the chase. Today the once splendid Durlach has become a mere suburb of Karlsruhe. Its shape, however, still betrays the original plan of the shanty town, which extended only southwards from the accurately oriented star of radiating rides. To the north the hunting grounds, with here and there an ancient hunter's hut, lie undisturbed in the lonely forest, while behind them lie the game preserve, fishing canals, zoological enclosure and gardens. We receive a vivid impression of the proportion of land devoted to the baroque hunt—forming in this particular case the nucleus of a big modern town. The circumstance did not escape the sharp tongue of Liselotte von der Pfalz, who in one of her letters wrote of the young prince, in her judgement an ill-bred crank, as a 'paper-mad fool' and a 'spider on a grand scale'. One anecdote illustrates the role of the hunting ground in the foundation of new towns: the prince returned from the hunt hot and exhausted, only to find that one of his favourites had lost her valuable fan in the forest. He rode out once more to look for it, but fell asleep under a tree. In his dreams he still thought of fans, and in a confused poetic way conceived the idea of a fan-shaped city. On waking, he could hardly wait to draw up the plans of his dream town.

Riding to hounds in pursuit of the deer was the kind of chase most favoured by the baroque courts, but the less ceremonial hunting of smaller woodland creatures took up a not inconsiderable part of their time. An exhaustive survey of the different hunting methods and species of game fashionable at that time was written in the first half of the eighteenth century by Johann Elias Riedinger, whose charming and expert commentaries are still of interest to sportsmen today. The forms of hunting he describes were practised in high society and court circles up to the beginning of the twentieth century. Most German princes had exchanged the mounted hunt for the more comfortable shooting of game driven within the range of their guns by beaters. There was also the shooting of small game such as pheasants and hares, which was a more private and intimate affair untrammeled by court ceremonial. The special method of hunting the deer most repugnant to our modern sense of fair play was the 'water hunt', in which the quarry was chased into a water-filled basin from which there was no escape and where the terrified beasts could be slaughtered with ease from the opposite bank.

Only princes and noblemen possessed hunting rights, and their passion for the sport weighed heavily on the local tenant farmers and foresters. Not only was it part of their statute labour to beat up game for the lord, but they were not allowed to protect their land from the favourite objects of the chase, who were allowed to destroy their crops unhindered. A heavy penalty was exacted from any peasant or townsman who shot one of the pests. At the end of the eighteenth century the farmers of the Ansbach region had to watch their fields day and night to drive away the hungry deer with loud alarms. In the same area one district comprising 200 hamlets suffered annual damage amounting to 150,000 gulden, a loss of nearly half the expected yield.

A perceptive report on the consequences of the aristocratic passion for hunting was written by the critical economist and chronicler of Wurtemberg, Albrecht von Haller. According to him, the Dukedom of Wurtemberg could have supported many more inhabitants if the Duke's amusements had not sequestered such a large area of forest and so great an animal population within it. Haller wrote that 'wild boars, fallow and other deer wander at will and afraid of no one until St. Hubert's day, when hundreds of them are slaughtered. These animals do a great deal of damage to the grain fields, but may not be shot.'

Some idea of the enormous extent of hunting and shooting there can be gained by the huge 'bags' obtained. In a single state shooting party held in 1748 no fewer than 5,000 head of game were slaughtered.

The burden laid on the almost rightless villein farmers by the princely hunts quickly became a symbol of general oppression in the later days of absolute rule. This is made very clear in a passage by Matthias Claudius, supposedly written by a hunted stag to the prince that had pursued him.

'Serene Highness, my gracious lord and duke, I have this day had the honour of being hunted by Your Serene Highness's hounds. I most humbly beseech Your Grace graciously to spare me that pain in future. If Your Serene Highness were so hunted but once, he would not find my plea so unreasonable. I lie here unable to lift my head, blood streams from my mouth and nostrils. How can Your Serene Highness find it in his heart to hunt to death an innocent beast that feeds only on grass and herbs? It may be that Your Serene Highness finds pleasure in the chase, but if he knew how my heart beats he would surely forbear.

I have the honour to remain your faithful servant till death,'

In the guise of the harmless, innocent creature whose suffering is caused by the hunting Duke's quest for pleasure, he represents the plight of the oppressed peasantry, deprived of its just rights and degraded to a plaything for the Duke's amusement. Concealed in the popular form of an animal fable

14 *Fontainebleau: detail from the wall of Napoleon's bedroom. After the destruction of the interior by the revolutionaries in 1789, the palace was restored to its former glory during the First Empire. To legitimise his imperial claims Napoleon associated himself with the traditional seat of the French kings, and had the despoiled apartments redecorated in the fashion of the day, the Empire Style named after him. In some cases the elegant, classical decoration overlaid or replaced the florid wall-coverings and furniture of the reigns of François I and his successors. Following the example of the kings of France, especially Louis XIV, whose sun emblem was everywhere visible, he had his initial N, surrounded by the laurel wreath of victory, displayed wherever it was most likely to catch the eye. The comparatively austere lines and limited colour range of the new style were based on models from classical Rome and Greece, as well as ancient Egypt. Among the favourite symbols were accordingly genies, sphinxes, gryphons, pseudo-antique medallions, palm fronds, garlands of fruit, and tasselled fringes.*

15 *Fontainebleau: Napoleon's bedroom decorated in the first decade of the 19th century. The yearning to identify with the French monarchy of the* grand siècle *was especially noticeable in the furnishings of his bedroom, far too exuberant for the taste of the period, with its splendidly canopied bed of state. Although its references to the bedroom of the Sun King are almost explicit, Napoleon's apartment was mainly for show. His biographers tell us that, like Frederick the Great, his simple camp bed travelled with him wherever he went, to all the palaces from Paris to Vienna and Moscow, and from Fontaine-bleau to Rome.*

was a critical attitude expressing the growing opposition of the Age of Enlightenment, even though still in oracular style. The apparent devotion with which the injured beast humbly asks his tormentor for protection shimmers with irony, but the passage also points very clearly to the position of an oppressed class that was soon to rise and overturn with word and deed the feudal power of the nobility.

The Servants

We have not yet mentioned the staff needed to service the gigantic, inflated monster of ceremony and festival represented by a baroque court. On that subject too figures and dependable estimates remain as evidence. The figures also give a plausible explanation of the increasing size of palaces, princely residences and mansions, that had been growing more and more enormous ever since the Renaissance. It was a spiral: the buildings had to expand to represent the boundless power and magnificence of the ruling caste; to maintain these establishments huge staffs of servants and minor officers were required; further architectural expansion was necessary to provide room for their household functions and living quarters. And so the unbridled growth of baroque residences continued.

The tendency already apparent in medieval feudalism and the courts of the Renaissance now came into full flower: conspicuous consumption and vicarious idleness as a social symbol of the governing class. Freedom from productive labour was the mark of the nobleman and courtier. Leisure was exclusive to aristocratic life, productive work the sign of poverty and subjection. The activities—all unproductive, of course—that were considered appropriate to the higher ranks of society became ever more select. Government, war, religion, sport, play and hunting strictly as an amusement, were among the 'permitted' and favourite occupations at court. As a further refinement they were embellished by minor social accomplishments and arts. One of these, almost a science in itself, was keeping up with the swiftly changing fashion in clothes. Others were polite conversation, gallant deportment with the fair sex and good manners at table and in bed. Very important was correct behaviour in the court of honour, at the hunt or while trundling a hoop, or playing at battledore and shuttlecock, card games, chess or dice. These accomplishments had to be studied under a highly qualified professional if one wanted to keep up to date. That included, of course, training in the arts of fencing, riding and dancing, as well as perfect deportment on the duelling ground, in the riding school and in the ballroom.

While the enormous palaces of the baroque nobility, the monstrous luxury of their games and festivals, eating and drinking, clothes, footwear, hairdressing, and the ornateness of their furniture, coaches, saddlery and dress swords, all bore witness to their power, wealth and social superiority, there grew up at the same time the concept of idleness as not so much a right as a duty. But leisure itself could become so entangled with complications and etiquette as almost to amount to work, though at least useless work. Even that was not enough. Many aristocratic landowners could afford conspicuous consumption and idleness. The monarch and his court must make their superiority clear: there must be servants to stand idle by proxy. Among the palace staff of the baroque age that principle was raised to a fine art. Footmen in coloured livery grew numb beside double doorways in case anyone should wish to pass through, waited all day in the courtyard to open the doors of the few carriages that might drive in, froze in sentry-boxes at the entrance to the park to present arms two or three times daily. All these were proof of the

44

sovereign's absolute pre-eminence. Others could afford leisure; he could afford to let others be idle in his stead.

Apart from the court officials charged with governmental and administrative duties, the machinery of display and ceremonial required a great multitude of employees and servants. At a great court the numbers approached those of an army; at a minor court they were often out of all proportion to the actual political and economic power of the petty princeling at its head.

Thus the imperial household in Vienna had a staff of 2,000 servants and officials. Like an army in the field they were split up into divisions, in this case six: the departments headed by the Chief Steward, the Lord Chamberlain, the Lord Chief Marshal, the Master of Horse, the Chief Ranger and the Head Falconer respectively. In addition, the various members of the imperial family each had their own households. The Empress had the largest after the Emperor, then the Archdukes and Archduchesses and so on down the family in order of rank, the staffs amounting to thousands of serving men and women in all. The exchequer of the Vienna court had to support an estimated 25,000 people, the population of a large town in baroque reckoning. Kayssler, a travel writer reporting from Australia in 1730, calculated that the number of imperial household servants in the whole of the Emperor's dominions came to about 40,000, and we have no reason to doubt his word.

The Emperor had fifteen sons of the nobility to wait on him personally. The boys' education and care required the employment of no fewer than 5 tutors, 2 dancing masters, 1 fencing master, 8 servants, 4 cooks, 1 steward and 1 preceptor, amounting to 22 persons in all. In her stables the Empress Maria Theresia kept 2,200 highly bred horses. A stable staff of 400 men was employed for their maintenance. During her reign the personal household establishment in the imperial palaces was 1,500 strong.

Since the minor potentates modelled their courts on those at Vienna and Versailles, they too had to have their levées and high tables in the Sun King manner. Even the most insignificant margrave maintained a punctilious court and reproduced all the household offices customary in Vienna and Versailles, even if only one half or third as many as those august examples. There were chamberlains, grooms of the bedchamber, Lord High Marshals, Masters of Ceremony, Masters of the Horse, Chief Rangers, messengers and so on more than enough to maintain their state.

17

17 Paris, Louvre: the east front. The contribution of the 17th century, France's grand siècle, to the mixed architectural styles of the Louvre, that perpetual royal building site, was its most significant one in relation to European architecture and stylistic history as a whole. In 1665 the King himself summoned the leading master builder of Rome, the Cavalier Gianlorenzo Bernini, to Paris to produce plans and models for the east and end facades in situ. Bernini's plans, however, ran into insuperable difficulties, partly due to

18

differences in national taste and partly to the jealous intrigues of established French architects. Claude Perrault got the commission in the end and carried it out in 1667–1671. His conception gains a dignified vitality from the long colonnade of paired Corinthian columns set above an exceptionally high podium. The vertical line of the columns is relieved by the contrasting middle section with its gabled pediment and by the slightly protruding cornices that frame the colonnade.

18 Paris, Louvre: Part of the façade. The palace suffered severely dring the Paris Commune of 1871. Some sections that had been burnt to the ground were rebuilt in the original baroque style during subsequent years. The illustration shows one of the reconstructed wings.

Page 50:
19 Paris, Louvre: the Richelieu pavilion. This section was added to the old palace during the reign of Napoleon III (1852–1870) in the style of the Second Empire (like that of the Paris Opera House). Although the proportions and scale of the baroque original have been borne in mind, this pompus and theatrical composition is interesting only historically as one stratum in the many-layered architectural medley of the Louvre, and stands out from the rest like a sore thumb.

Politics and the Arts
in the Age of Absolutism

France

State Religion

A characteristic mark of absolute rule is the secularization of the ritual functions hitherto performed by the Church. Court ceremonial partly replaces religious ritual, dominates and subordinates it. Simultaneously the hitherto undisputed, almost obligatory consultation with the Church on worldly politics falls into disuse. In the lands that had broken away from Catholicism (England, Scandinavia, the Protestant States-General of the Netherlands) the collapse of the Church's political power occurred quite early, but in arch-Catholic France it was delayed until the reign of Louis XIV. The process reached its logical conclusion in the revolution of 1789 with the complete secularization of the state. That would never have been possible without the preceding demythologising.

In the absolute State the Church fulfils a merely ornamental function: to adorn, instruct, educate and moralize. That brings her into a specific relationship with the State. Since the State controls the vital areas of economy, policy and culture, the Church has necessarily to toe the line. She becomes a 'state church', subordinate to national and worldly power. In the case of France, she was not primarily responsible to the Pope and Rome but to the absolute monarch and his state ideology. Finally, the Church declines into a component of the establishment's prestige, the apotheosis of the ruler, on a level with other state adornments. The situation prepared the way for the complete separation now existing in France. The mother church of Rome steadily lost ground as a factor in government and a supervisor of morals.

Certain events in French ecclesiastical history are symptomatic of this long, slow decline. Since no one and nothing could be allowed to disturb or obfuscate the central, well-defined and unified position of the state church as a means of increasing and exalting the worldly power of the state, ruthless war was waged on all religious divergents, especially the French Protestants, to deprive them of all political power. The history of the non-Catholic sects of France is written in blood and tears, and finally led to mass flights of almost modern dimensions, comparable to the mass emigrations and expulsions that occurred just before and after the Second World War. Following the foundation of the Reformed Church in Geneva by the Frenchman Calvin in 1536 Calvinism spread quickly over France. In the Huguenot movement it achieved a socially, economically and intellectually superior organisational form that tended towards autonomy. The growth of capitalism was indissolubly linked with the Calvinist doctrine of predestination and the rewarding in this life of the God-fearing with worldly prosperity. Huguenots adopted the Calvinist belief that work was a guarantee against sin (a variation of the old monastic principle *Ora et Labora*) and hence that idleness was a precondition of sin. Since the Calvinist ideal of life was a puritanical and ascetic one, profit was not to be used for personal luxury, and therefore entered a spiral of investment and more profit. It was the beginning of an accumulation of capital in the modern sense, which in England, for example, soon gave rise to capitalistic phenomena.

Calvinism of the Huguenot type was also the driving force of the earliest movements of middle class emancipation. In France religious argument became involved with current party political disputes, and these visibly

Pages 54–55:
20 *Versailles: the east front and great forecourt (court of honour) designed by Louis Le Vau in 1661–1670. On the right, the Chapel Royal, part of the north wing built by Le Vau's successor (1668–1703). It stands out above the surrounding buildings by virtue of its high, gabled roof. The two pavilions along each side of the inner court of honour, finished off with two charmingly classical triangular pediments above rows of huge Corinthian columns, are 18th century additions dating from the time of Gabriel, the Court Architect-in-Chief. The photograph gives an idea of the size and magnificence of the inner and outer courts of honour, which were the setting of so many grand ceremonies of welcome. The wide perspective gradually narrows, guiding the eye towards the dominating centre of the façade, where the king's bedroom was located. The whole splendid, if somewhat stiff, architectural scene is an expression rendered in stone of the French absolute monarchy's pretensions to glory.*

assumed a radical, and anti-monarchist colour. Two very different groups, united only in their common foe, had set themselves in opposition to a subordinated yet paramount church, and so, to some extent, to the crown itself. These were the Holy League, a Rome-oriented, Catholic organisation headed by the noble house of Guise, and the Huguenots, a Protestant folk movement. Both groups were ambitious for power, in the former case even absolute power. The Huguenot opposition, in the form of a broad-based revolt, held the seeds of revolution; the leaders of the Holy League, the Guise family, put forward dynastic claims to the throne in a monarchically centralized state.

This early theory of civic emancipation and the right to resist a tyrannical monarch, clearly derived from Calvin's ideas, was first championed by Calvin's successor Theodor Beza and later by the Jesuit Mariana.

The long and increasingly fierce altercation eventually that occurred between 1562 and 1598 turned into military action and came to a head in the St. Bartholomew's Night massacre of 1572 when, in Paris and the surrounding neighbourhood, thousands of leading Huguenots were treacherously murdered. When Henri IV came to the throne he issued an Edict of Tolerance at Nantes (1598) which guaranteed the Huguenots freedom of conscience, a limited freedom to practise their religion and a 'safe area' (La Rochelle!), thus ending the appalling religious strife. The State finally granted a degree of civic and religious emancipation to establish the House of Bourbon on the throne in the person of Henri IV, formerly a Protestant himself. Tolerance was the price that had to be paid for the sake of peace and undisputed government.

The Edict of Nantes may have been a clever move to create a unified, national state of France, something that could not exist in an atmosphere of religious struggle. A hundred years later, however, in the high noon of Absolutism, the dynamic Huguenots had once more become economically powerful and independent enough to make inroads on the absolute, autocratic might of the crown. In 1685 Louis XIV, with unparalleled cynicism, revoked the Edict of Nantes. Cardinal Richelieu had already destroyed the Huguenots' refuge of La Rochelle as early as 1628. Later the Protestants were harassed by having troops perpetually billeted on them, the so-called *dragonades*. The revocation set off a mass flight of about half a million Huguenots. Many became refugees abroad, especially in Holland and Brandenburg. As so many of them had held key posts in commerce and were skilled in science and handicrafts, their loss did serious damage to French economy. It was thought of as a fair exchange for the restoration of a single creed and a unified Catholic Church under state control.

The National Council of Paris (1682) ratified the idea of a French state church with absolute rights: the king possessed the 'right of instruction' in the matter of filling the high ecclesiastical offices, and by the so-called Gallican Articles even had a right of veto on papal decisions.

During the last years of Louis XIV's reign, from 1710 onwards, the State continued its repressive policy with the persecution of the Jansenists—named after C. Jansenius, Bishop of Ypres—who advocated a reform of the Church from within, a return to the original Christian beliefs and the 'pure' teaching of the Early Father, St. Augustine. Inevitably, the movement took on an anticlerical tinge. Its headquarters was the convent at Port Royal, situated at Versailles—an unbearable provocation to the king, who had grown pious in his old age.

No wonder, then, that France joined in the persecution of the Jesuits, although there, in the more reasonable atmosphere of an enlightened age, it did not assume such an inhumane and repressive form as in Spain and Italy.

21 *Versailles: the main west garden façade was added to Le Vau's original wing in the 1680s by Hardouin-Mansart, who enclosed the inner terrace to create enough room for the Hall of Mirrors. The centre of the frontage, which also marks the centre of the Hall of Mirrors, is distinguished by a row of six mighty Ionic columns. In front of the garden façade stretches a great terrace, leading down immensely wide steps to the park with its flower-beds and ornamental waters. The garden terrace lifts the palace itself to a dominating height above the garden, yet acts as a transition area between mansion and park.*

The relation of Church to State is made particularly clear in the subordination of the sacred precincts within the royal residence to the palace as a whole.

Unquestionably the chapel at Versailles is a magnificent, separate and artistically decorated apartment, but it is by no means in the central position one might expect, being pushed out to one side of the entrance courtyard. It is very little larger than the court opera house or the rooms of state. As already indicated, morning prayers in the royal chapel were not the high point of the day's routine, but one ceremonial performance among others. The turning of the courtiers towards the king rather than the altar is significant. Altars were of lesser importance than the monarch. Contemporary state philosophy was able to justify the situation. For instance, Jacques Bossuet, Louis XIV's court chaplain till 1704, provided an impressive formula for the ascendancy of absolute princes over all the powers of this world with the phrase *Un Roi, une foi, une loi* (One king, one faith, one law), signifying that the monarch, as earthly representative of the Divine Ruler, was accountable only to the Deity, not to the Church, and certainly not to the people. And insofar as he represented the one and only valid law, he was of course above all ecclesiastical laws, an extraordinary change when compared to medieval ideas.

With this background it is no wonder that the terrestial ruler's central position in the church was even symbolised by the placing of the royal sun emblem in the centre of the west window in Orléans Cathedral.

Much more than a century later a similar act of occupation and usurpation took place—though from different motives and in a provincial backwater— when the Dukes of Leiningen were awarded the town and monastery of Amorbach during the period of secularization. The new owners glorified

57

22

themselves by displaying their coat-of-arms on the high altar of the abbey church, and even more conspicuously on the high altar above the emblem of the Holy Trinity, and not as they could well have done in some more modest place such as the organ screen. It was a last and utterly anachronistic echo of absolute sovereignty.

The tendency is equally evident in another type of 18th century residence, in this case Würzburg Palace, the seat of a spiritual ruler, the Prince Bishop. There too the chapel does not occupy a central position, but is situated in a pavilion in a side wing, where it does not appear to rank above any other pavilion. Strolling along the front of the building, one would have to look close to identify its function. Nor is its size much greater than that of the great entrance hall. It would almost seem as if in baroque court society of the absolutist era the ritual of the staircase and kneeling before the earthly ruler took precedence over concern with the heavenly hierarchy and kneeling before one's God. Although (admittedly in allegorical and highly ornamental form) the Christian religious subject matter in the palace's picture gallery still occupies a central place, in equal competition with Olympian and mythological scenes.

The extent of the change, the secularization of spiritual and ecclesiastical power is manifest when one compares Versailles, or even Würzburg, with a palace of equal political and artistic rank in the 16th century, namely the Escorial, begun by Philip I in 1563 and completed in 1584, the focal point of the Spanish Hapsburg monarchy in the late Renaissance. The dominating centre of the whole, great complex is the church of the San Lorenzo monastery.

'One must compare Versailles with the Escorial in order to understand the differences of belief between the kingdoms of France and Spain at the

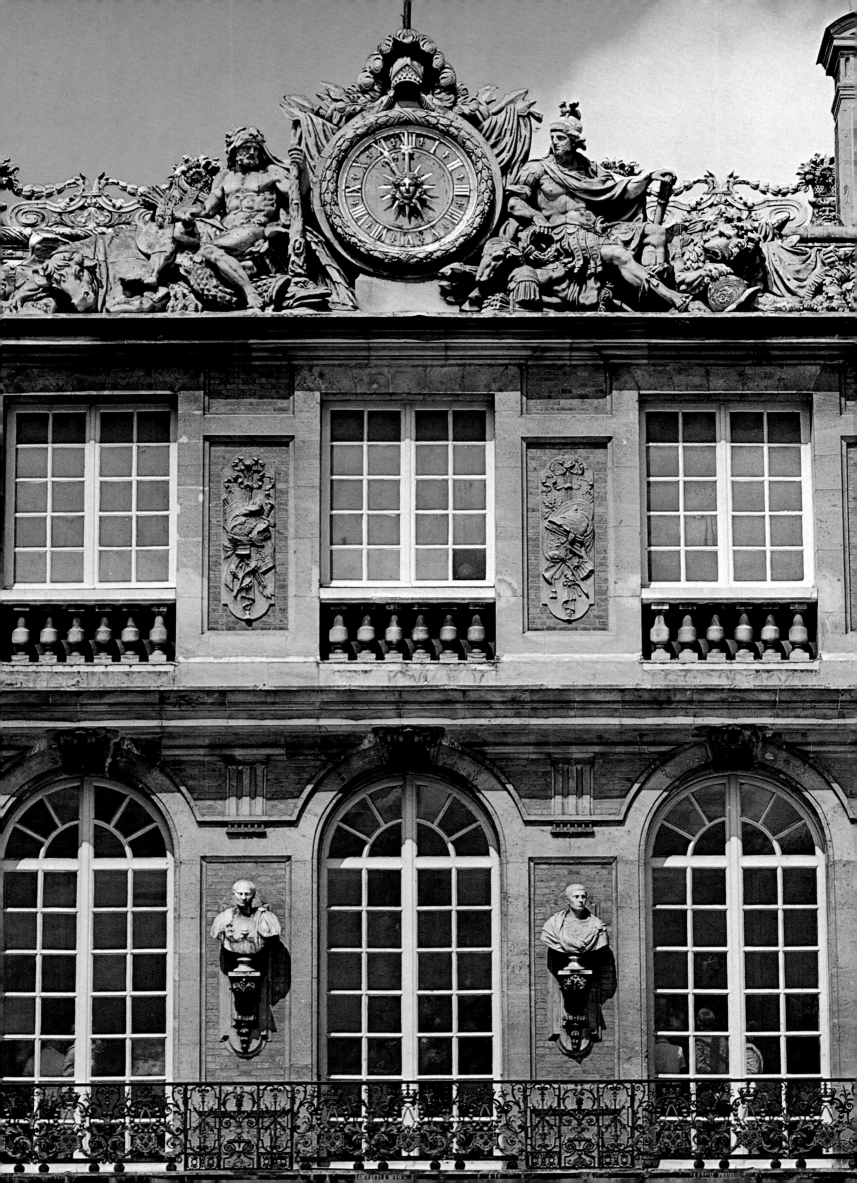

summits of their power. In Versailles the royal bedchamber, in which the king, like the sun, rises and goes to rest, is the heart of the palace. The chapel is pushed to one side. In the Escorial the royal apartments surround the basilica. It is made plain that worldly power must be founded on orthodoxy and piety.'

(Braunfels)

The Administration of the State

States of the pre-absolute, feudal era were supported by a loosely knit, administratively undeveloped staff of officials that came into office more or less by chance, served when required and did not as yet act independently.

The administrative needs of the absolute state, however, grew at a breathtaking speed and demanded an altogether better organised, more consistent management possessing greater technical skill in methods of government. Bureaucracy blossomed, a process that has by no means faded away today. In fact, we are in no position to mock the grotesque growth of officialdom in the age of absolutism. We may smile when we read in old records that in the late 18th century even dog kennels were not exempt from the control and enquiries of all-powerful officialdom in petty German princedoms (in Öttingen they wanted to know the 'name, breed, use and outward appearance of every dog within the princely territories'); or that in Gernsheim in 1776 the police fined anyone who 'crossed the street with a tobacco pipe in his mouth' 10 kreuzers, anyone who 'climbed a garden fence' 20 kreuzers, and anyone whose 'cart drove against the side of the road or over a gutter' 24 kreuzers. But *plus ça change, plus c'est la même chose*. We still have our experts on dog licences and statistics of the pet population, fines for a multitude of different traffic offences, and detailed income tax and social security forms to fill in that are no less complicated than corresponding ordinances under the rule of French or German absolute monarchs.

As the grip of the State tightened on the purse and person of its every citizen, the need arose for a differentiated, thoroughly organised civil service. For the absolute State, with its immense external and internal expenditure, on palaces at home and military adventures abroad, was supported on the shoulders—in other words, the purses—of its subjects.

In establishing a court of exchequer, the *chambre de compte*, Philippe IV, the 'counterfeiting King', had already taken a decisive step towards a policy of centralized state finance and administration. Under Henri IV and his talented minister Sully the same policy continued into the 17th century, with a tighter control over agriculture and finance.

Jean Bodin's doctrine of the State's sovereignty, laid out in the treatise *Six Livres de la République* (1576), and Thomas Hobbes' theory of the State contract, elaborated in *Leviathan* (1651) were put to practical use in the internal policies of the 17th century. The ever more independent governmental administration was considered to be justified by the theory that in the chaotic situation of early mankind the only rule of life had been all against all. Therefore, to survive, men were forced to transfer their natural rights—with no possibility of retracting—to the State, to be exercised undividedly, indissolubly and unquestioned over all its subjects, and requiring a perfectly organized administration to light up every corner of the social structure.

The old representative systems of government were in opposition to centralized administration, the exclusive rights of the nobility and absolute power in the person of the sovereign or in court institutions set up by him. Accordingly, they had been eroded little by little, starting as early as the reign of Louis XIII, whose chief minister, Cardinal Richelieu, gradually took over their powers and set royally appointed officials in their place. It was not yet possible, however, wholly to suppress the traditional purchase of certain posts, or the existence of local councils or *parlements*.

Disputes between the crown and these *parlements*, especially the leading one of Paris, marked the years of the regency which was in command during the minority of Louis XIV.

He had been born to Louis XIII and his queen after twenty-two years of marriage. Out of gratitude for the birth of an heir, his parents called the baby prince 'Louis Dieudonné' and erected a special church Val-de-Grace, in his honour on the left bank of the Seine. Only five years later he came to the throne. His mother, Anne of Austria, became the nominal regent, but the real power was vested in the great Italian Cardinal Mazarin, head of the Royal Council.

During this interregnum without a dynastic leader in command, the French crown was in greater peril than at any previous time in its history. The king was a child. New, dangerous, even revolutionary ideas were abroad, especially in England, and threatened to engulf the continent. The danger, not only to the State but also to his person, must have made an ineradicable impression on Louis during his childhood. It explains certain momentous traits in the character of the adult king. Without that personal experience the evolution of the absolute monarchy in France might have been less pervasive, less repressive and less complete.

The opening chapters in the story of the totalitarian Ludovician State are largely taken up by disputes between the regent, Queen Anne, and her minister Mazarin on one side and the people and *parlement* of Paris on the other, in which the survival of the traditional French monarchy aad the 'little king were at stake The only alternative for the royal family was emigration or death. Final victory laid the foundation stone of the absolute State—and incidentally the foundation stone of that State's highest cultural achievement, namely Versailles. In 1661 Cardinal Mazarin died and Louis XIV became master in his own house. In 1663 he commissioned the architect Le Vau and the garden designer Le Notre to turn Louis XIII's hunting lodge into the palace and park of Versailles as we know them today.

It could be maintained that France was ripe for revolution more than a 100 years before it eventually broke out in 1789, that is to say in the middle of the 17th century, in the days of the Fronde and the struggle between the central power of the throne and the *parlement*.

The Paris *parlement* was a visible expression of divided power, a safeguard against the perversion of monarchy to tyranny, rule by force, and absolute power. As an assembly of individuals versed in law, it was capable of making laws, criticizing and controlling them. According to tradition, royal edicts and regulations were laid before *parlement*, where they could be discussed or even annulled.

At this time the fierce English Civil War of 1642–1649, led by Cromwell, had not long ended. The conflict between Crown and Parliament, between the trend towards absolute monarchy and the Puritan rule of the people, had come into the open. The English example affected France: the people and council of Paris demanded more rights, only to be sternly refused by Mazarin. So they organized resistance in the so-called Fronde. In 1648, the era of the Westphalian Peace, many of the leading Frondists and members of parliament were arrested. That arbitrary action sparked the flame of rebellion. Barricades were erected in the streets of Paris, as so often in her subsequent history. At first the regency council appeared conciliatory: taxes were reduced, political prisoners unjustly arrested by means of royal *lettres de cachet* were released, tax proposals were to be submitted to *parlement*.

LUSTRE LOUIS XV.
DONATION DE
MADAME ARTURO LOPEZ-WILLSHAW
ET DU BARON ALEXIS DE REDÉ 1966

26

25 *Versailles: Louis XIV's bedroom in the middle section of the old palace, as it is today. It was altered and extended by Mansart in the early 17th century. Here, morning after morning, the ceremonial rising of the king took place in the presence of crowds of courtiers. and here, in 1715, he died. The bust by Coysevox on the chimneypiece is an ideal portrait of Louis XIV, model for so many portraits of princes with similar aspirations in the years to come. The beautiful chandelier reflected in the mirror is from the reign of Louis XV.*

26 *The tapestry depicting the entry of Alexander the Great into Babylon was made from a giant painting by the chief court artist Le Brun, now at the Louvre. The intended parallel between Alexander and Louis is obvious. As head of the realm, world statesman, founder of colonies, absolute monarch and warlord for whom frontiers were no barrier, the king felt himself the equal of the ancient world-conqueror.*

Valuable time was gained in which to encircle the citizens of Paris. The Prince de Condé was chosen to be the saviour of his country. While the royal family withdrew to St. Germain, the Prince's troops formed a ring round the city and laid siege to it. For three months gunsmoke hung over the streets of the capital. In the end Condé went over to the Frondist side and, to the great joy of the people, that hated 'foreigner', Mazarin, was temporarily driven from the country. The rebellion itself, however, was not successful. As in the days of the Huguenots, it was a forced marriage between a popular movement and a nobles' revolt. There was too much disunity in their ranks, too many contradictory aims, for the rebels to be able to anticipate the reforms of 1789 or realize the optimistic libertarian ideals of the Renaissance, Humanism and an Utopian parliamentarianism. Consequently, the central power of the monarchy emerged the stronger for its battle with the Fronde and established a totalitarian State by reinforcing and enlarging all the royal privileges already in existence.

Mazarin's death in 1661 marked the birth of absolute power in France, and the undivided sovereignty of the young king. The ministers of state were dismissed, there was no further mention of the *Etats Generaux*, the consultative body that had not been summoned since 1614, when Richelieu came to power. Now the King was undisputed head of the secret Council of State; there was no one to question his decisions or control his edicts. The parliament of Paris was degraded to the rank of a provincial court and lost all power of appeal. Louis dismissed and arrested the once mighty Fouquet, Minister of Finance and Taxation, and took the administration of national law, finance and taxation into his own hands. He was the living Law; he, himself, was the State, as declared in his boastful motto *L'Etat, c'est moi*.

Perhaps it is hardly surprising that his youthful anxieties and his long sojourn in the gloomy old stronghold of the Louvre, not any too safe from the aggressive Parisian populace, led to a change of cultural and architectural policy. Proud and stubborn, the King turned his back on 'his' town, to which he never felt he belonged, to build his own architectural crystal, a focus for all the light in the kingdom, and from which the light of the crown and his majestic person would radiate. That central crystal was Versailles, the ultimate symbol of the absolute State.

The royal provincial and city councils functions at a very low administrative level, while the landed nobility, the seigneurs, were deprived of most of their authority and local rights of arrest. Centrally controlled financial authorities called *chambres* took the place of the old chancellories. Law courts, councils of war and ecclesiastical councils completed the web of administration. An ever more powerful police organisation multiplied to supervise every aspect of the citizen's life. The concept of 'policing' was not the equivalent of a modern police force's duties of protection and crime investigation, but covered every kind of state administration. As a result the nation became a 'police state' based on almost universal surveillance of everyone and everything by practically everybody.

Since the holders of administrative authority were increasingly drawn from the 'new classes', the minor nobility and the rising burghers, and since they possessed no feudal landed property, there grew up a loyal Pretorian Guard that had exchanged the sword for the goose quill, the lance for the ruler, the heroic epic for exact figures in the ledgers. With that armoury they devised as ruthless a machine for oppression as the feudal lords of the Middle Ages and Renaissance.

In this field the 18th century saw an unfortunate perversion. The French example found fruitful soil in the petty princedoms of Germany and Austria and flourished exceedingly:

'It is significant that, in the absolute monarchies of the 18th century, police reporters and politicians regarded the whole of the nation's economic and financial organisation as a legitimate field of police activity. These writers and financial experts speak of agricultural police, hunt police, fishery, mountain, factory and trade police, even church and cultural police. The absolute state exerted so much pressure on these officials that they could only see economic and cultural activities as matters for police surveillance.'

(Kampfmeyer)

The independent judiciary was destroyed by every sort of inroad on its authority on the part of the king and his 'secret' councillors; interference with verdicts, royal warrants for arrests, arrest on suspicion of subversive political activity, which meant unlimited imprisonment in the Bastille, and finally the institution of secret police, whose duties were chiefly political spying and use of informers. All these measures sound sadly familiar to modern ears, although they were the inglorious achievements of French absolutism in the 17th and 18th centuries. However, they also nursed the seed of historical change: the storming of the Bastille, where the king's untried prisoners languished, heralded the great revolution of 1789.

The Military State

The absolute, centralized State, imbued with nationalistic ideas, needed successes abroad to justify its despotic power over the lives of all its subjects. So the reverse side of Louis XIV's 'peaceful' reign was military activity on a scale almost unprecedented in Europe. How successful Louis was as a warlord is not a matter within the scope of this book. We are only concerned with the fact that the military policy of France in the 'great century', with its battlefields spread over half Europe—in Germany, Spain, Savoy and northern Italy, and at sea off the French coast near La Hogue, required a war machine of hitherto unheard-of proportions and flawless efficiency. The backbone and driving force of all this fighting apparatus was the standing army. What was new about the military organisation of Absolutism? Let us glance back into military history to get a standard of comparison.

The first 'modern' armies were the mercenary troops of the late 15th century and the whole of the 16th century. They did better in battle than the clumsy mounted knights of the Middle Ages with their great carapaces of clanking metal and their limited mobility, being superior not only in weapons but also practically and tactically. The destruction of the last great army of medieval cavalry under Charles the Bold of Burgundy by the nimble Swiss mercenary foot soldiers is a well known example (1476–77). They could infiltrate the enemy lines like weasels in a poultry yard.

The mercenaries shared three distinctive characters. They were hired soldiers working for a wage; they were highly qualified experts in the crafts of war; as craftsmen and wage-earners they were—like members of a guild—democratically organised. A mercenary army squad—the smallest military unit—elected one of themselves as 'general sergeant' to act as its representative even in dealing with their own captain, and as their attorney in the case of a court-martial. They were no heroes, but professional soldiers who sold their lives as dearly as possible in what was often the only trade they could pursue in such hard times. There were occasions when they refused to fight. The reason was neither cowardice nor fear of the enemy's superiority, but annoyance at discovering their pay to be noticeably lower than that of the opposing side—also mercenaries. Thus, at the battle of Marignano in 1515, the Swiss were furious to discover that their German opponents and colleagues earned nearly as much as they did, while in the following year

28

27, 28   Versailles: the Chapel Royal (view of
the choir and vaulted ceiling). This harmonious and distinguished interior, perhaps
the most beautiful in Versailles, was commissioned in 1688 by the Sun King and completed
in 1703 from plans by Mansart. Mass was
celebrated here every morning in the presence
of the whole court, who were obliged to turn
their regard towards the king, while he alone

faced the altar, almost on a level, so to speak
with the divine Sovereign. In this setting, with
its original synthesis of classical and medieval
(Corinthian pillars and soaring vault) the
ageing, increasingly pious Sun King appeared
full of dignity, without undue pomp. The
colour scheme of the white architectural
features with the painted and gilded ceiling
(by Antoine Coypel, 1708) is unforgettable.

Maximilian's German troops mutinied because after their victory there their wages had still not been raised to the Swiss mercenaries' level.

In the same way, the renaissance army captain was at once military expert and businessman, having to calculate not only trajectories but also wages and costs.

'A renowned artilleryman and gunner was in much the same position as a modern specialist in armament manufacture, working one day for an English firm and another for an American one. Mercenary generals, too, although purely soldiers, could be compared to the international engineering experts of today. Famous commanders-in-chief such as the Spaniards, Gonsalvo de Cordova and Pedor de Novarra, considered themselves not so much chivalric warriors as military specialists whose chief business was to use their skills for profit. The upright German commander, Georg von Frundsberg, was basically a wholesale contractor for the mustering and maintenance of hired armies. He worked on speculation and, in fact, eventually lost his fortune.'

(H. Schulz)

With fighting so much a commercial transaction, the soldier can hardly be expected to have had much national spirit. At the most, he preferred to fight for his own country rather than against it.

Under the rule of the French absolute monarchy, however, with the consolidation of the state and its power over the individual, the situation changed fundamentally. There arose a strictly organised national army based on the soldier's unquestioning obedience, but not weighed down with great overheads of wages. It was a standing army. That is to say, a proportion of the state's military forces was permanently maintained under arms, not only to be instantly available in case of an emergency, but also as a guarantee of the king's power. If war broke out the army could quickly be brought up to full strength. Links had long existed between sections of the fighting forces and certain powerful feudal lords, who were obliged to supply the king with a certain number of knights and footsoldiers. These men tended to be primarily loyal to their overlords and had not infrequently been used against the central power. It was plainly in the interest of the absolute State to break those links, so that the army should be attached only to the State, while the State was personified in the monarch, who thus became absolute head of his army. With the object of strengthening the national state, Philippe IV had carried through some innovations at the expense of feudal power: he replaced the traditional feudal service of raising a levy by the payment of a sum of money, and used the money to pay hired troops, whom he considered more reliable. Under Charles VII during the Hundred Years' War, the trend continued: in 1438 he arranged to pay for a standing army from the yield of the royal estates and in 1439 he divided the army into small 'ordinance companies' stationed all over France—the first instance of military-topographical organisation in the modern sense.

In Louis XIV's reign a true standing army was established. The enormous funds required to finance it were supplied through the national economy of the absolute State. The man who reformed the French army was the king's talented Minister for War, Louvois. From a population of 18,000,000 inhabitants he raised a conscripted force of 170,000 men, a huge proportion in the existing circumstances. There were other innovations: standard uniforms, improved and standardized weaponry, a functional division of the troops into infantry, artillery, cavalry, supply units and pioneers as well as a regular system of promotion. The king took most of his officers from the minor aristocracy without fortune, and paid his military officers according to much the same system as his government officials. He made sure of their loyalty with money and prizes.

29

Field Marshals Turenne, Gondé and Luxembourg welded the French army into the biggest and best in the world. Finally Vaubun, the ingenious military engineer, revolutionized fortification, perfecting the 'star fortress' with its six bastions and no blind spots, a device invented more than a century earlier, which completely changed the strategy of sieges and, indeed, of war. The army of the absolute State was not yet an army of the people as a whole. There was no universal conscription or military service. That came only with the revolution of 1789. However, a recruiting system by district was a first step.

Since every department of the absolute State was subject to the manipulation of income and capital, enterprise, profit and loss, it is hardly surprising to find the same thing in the standing army. Regular pay was necessary to its existence, and the funds for it could be raised by finely graded taxation according to class and income. The officers, however, thought it only their due as 'military officials' that they should make a little extra from perquisites. At the beginning, in the late 17th century, they were in charge of buying uniforms and arms for their troops. Through buying cheaply or skimping on materials, so that the soldiers' overcoats were too short or too thin, they could make a profit, and the less conscientious did so. Living quarters might be mean, rations inadequate or boots fall off the soldiers' feet before being renewed. The bad example of the French army in the 17th century was followed more than faithfully by Frederick the Great in Prussia in the late 18th century. A significant extract from the history of its uniforms tells how the waistcoats gradually shrunk into mere squares of cloth sewn on to the coat:

'The clothes funds were veritable gold mines for the *junker* officers. They cooked the accounts to the benefit of their own purses; they shortened the regulation coats, which saved them many yards of material. Their profit mania ate bit by bit into the soldiers' waistcoats: first the sleeves were cut off, and in the end all that was left was a little flap sewn on between the front edges of the coat. Shoes were another profitable item. "If Dido," wrote Lieutenant Rahmel, "carved a site for a town out of a cowshed, the captains plan to turn the company's boots into a couple of landed estates!" They cheated the peasants who provided forage for the cavalry horses, left the names of dead soldiers in the lists of the living and, for a military review, dragged the sick and wounded from hospital to fill up the gaps. There was no end to their tricks. Small wonder that the officers of Frederick's army were called "not soldiers but profiteering tradesmen".'

(*Lessing-Legende*, quoted by Wittfogel)

Whereas the mercenary fighter of the renaissance and early baroque period was his own contractor and had to fend for himself where arms and forage were concerned, a soldier under an absolute monarch had no rights and was expected to obey without question; a courageous bid to improve conditions might have endangered his very life. Both he and his officers had sworn fealty to the sovereign, and any internal criticism amounted to *lèse Majesté*, even high treason.

The new drill in Louis XIV's army was equally stupid and sadistic, an expression of contempt for the lower orders. The partially independent tactics of the mercenary armies were replaced by totally unified procedures on the field of battle. The men had to fight in closed squares even under artillery fire, often under the foolish command of unintelligent officers. The heartless concept of 'cannon fodder' arose and, for the first time in the modern history of war, tens of thousands of men could be slain in a single battle. Compared with that, the combats of the mercenary armies seem almost humane.

It was inevitable that such an army, at first perhaps inspired by a certain idealism and a growing sense of national identity, but later ever more

74

inefficiently led, corruptly administered, kept short of food, clothing and pay, badly treated and subjected to soul-destroying drill, should fall like chaff 'before the onslaught of the seething army of revolutionary France' (Wittfogel).

No walk of life was exempt from the organising tentacles of absolutism. Even Versailles was known as the 'courtiers' barracks'. The noble sycophants who were obliged to attend on the royal Presence lived in the cramped, badly heated, dimly lit guest rooms of the palace, deprived of every comfort and not much better than the living quarters of the *Grande Armée*. And like that army, they could not withdraw from their imposed duties. The mercenary soldiery of the 16th and 17th centuries could at least take to their heels, or even mutiny if pay or treatment was not right, without danger of execution, whereas the French soldiers could not leave their posts, even in peacetime, without being shot. In the same way, on a more elevated level, banishment from court, or the king's acceptance of a nobleman's offer to retire to one's comfortable country estate, was a sentence of social death. One instantly became an 'unperson'. The name of the unhappy recreant could only be whispered behind the hand, for fear the king or one of his omnipresent informers should hear it and be offended.

The courtiers' painful submissiveness sometimes took strange, even military forms. Contemporary reports tell us that once, when the fortunes of war were going badly, the king decided temporarily to have only bread and water served at his table, and insisted on his spoilt courtiers doing likewise, as a symbolic gesture of asceticism to show himself as the caring and careful father of his suffering people. In bad times the courtiers were not even allowed ink and paper, and ordered to save light and heat. To obtain money, silver and gold dishes and cutlery, some from the royal household, were thrown into the royal melting pot, while on the battlefield millions of gold pieces were dissipated on more or less pointless wars of prestige.

While the new national army adopted meaningless ritual and conventions that had no military value, life at court, with its iron-bound etiquette, began to assume an unmistakeably military tone. Indeed, the Sun King's morning parade through his Hall of Mirrors and past the bowing multitudes of courtiers was the counterpart to a military parade, though without the uniforms and weapons. The endless corridors that 'marched' from one end of the palace to the other, the disciplined hedgerows and militarily ordered lines of trees in the park of Versailles, could be taken as symbols of a regimented Nature and a totally regimented world, a paradigm of the soldiers of an absolutist State in their lines and squares, to whom the sovereign—as a contemporary anecdote relates—could give the orders for battle, through the persons of his company commanders, as 'You die here, you die there and you die there'.

The National Economy

When one considers the attainments and somewhat doubtful advances of the age of absolute monarchy, which nevertheless laid the foundations of today's regimented world, one is struck by the scale of the regime's organisation, achievements and display. The huge standing army, the ubiquitous administrative network, the burdens imposed by costly foreign adventures, long wars, enormous palaces, royal households, barracks, fortifications, etc.: where was all the money to come from in an era when the shameless exploitation of forced labour was no longer politically practicable?

The answer is that the modern type of state—as France already was in the *grand siècle*—could be run only on the basis of a planned and organised

national economy. The State itself was the all-embracing business enterprise, the absolute monarch its managing director, the minor nobility and higher officials acting as sub-contractors between court and populace.

The system used to finance this centralized state was state control of the economy. Without the production, accumulation, investment and realization of capital developed by that progressive system not one stone of Versailles would have been put on another, no hedge or tree would have been planted in the park, no canal dug, no fountain made to gush.

The enormous growth of expenditure on army and wars, administration, public utilities and buildings of state, royal establishments, culture, an efficient system of communications and government industries, demanded a regular and regulated influx of revenue to the state. While Colbert, the creator

31 *Versailles: the Basin of Apollo (*Bassin d'Apollon*) in the central avenue of the park designed in 1661 by the most famous garden architect of his day. André Le Notre. In the foreground the horse-drawn chariot of the sun god Apollo rises from 'the depths of the sea', facing east towards the rising sun and in direct line with the king's bedroom. Behind the basin stretches the 'tapis vert' (green carpet), a rectangle of lawn that extends nearly as far as the terrace steps. In the background we see the centre of the west garden front and the Hall of Mirrors.*

32

32 *Versailles: the* Bassin d'Apollon. *A nearer view of the group of allegorical statuary seen on the right of the previous ilustration. The stone waves and stylised dolphin head on the plinth relate the group to the ornamental water and Apollo fountain.*

of the economic system known as Colbertism, could not be said to have invented regular taxation, he had improved and polished it in connection with the modern principles of money economy and capitalism. As figurehead of the absolute State, the sovereign did not only take, as did the greedy princes of the Middle Ages and Renaissance, but also gave. This system of give and take, the principle of modern state economy, could be briefly summarized as follows: direct and indirect taxation levied on certain commodities, especially luxury goods, or on people, property or land, built up a stock of capital for the state in that most abstract and universal of all means of exchange: money, then symbolized by precious metals, either silver or gold. Since, however, the people and taxpayers could not be milked like cows for ever, a part of the taxes received was reinvested in the state enterprise to finance common undertakings. As competition with England grew sharper, Colbert put his trust in overseas trade, a successful colonial policy and—a prerequisite for those—a powerful merchant and fighting fleet. Therefore one of his first measures was to invest in national shipbuilding and encourage the construction and testing of new types of ship and an effective fighting navy.

Because a modern economy, an established commercial capitalism, needs a rapid, internal communication network, accessible at all seasons, for the distribution of goods, raw materials and labour forces, Colbert instituted an

33   Versailles: Grand Trianon on the edge of the Le Nôtre's park. It was erected to replace the Porcelain Trianon demolished in 1687 with a marble Trianon built from plans by Mansart and completed in 1688. The seclued mansion, enclosed in its garden world, was used by Louis XIV as a retreat from the fatiguing cares of state and ceremonial of the big palace. He enjoyed staying there with the love of his old age, Madame de Maintenon. The marble Trianon had its private garden, also designed by Le Nôtre. It included areas for botanical study, which greatly interested the king, as well as for useful vegetables (the royal kitchen garden or potager royal, *as it was called). Liselotte von der Pfalz preferred to spend her time there until her death in 1722. Louis XV, too, used the garden palace, but later created one of his own, the Petit Trianon. The Grand Trianon was renovated during the times of Napoleon and Louis Philippe. Finally it was radically restored by Charles de Gaulle and used as a government guest house.*

energetic policy of road-building. He had the old roads, which were dust tracks in summer and mud channels for the rest of the year, reinforced with rubble and cobblestones. Unreliable fords were bridged over and signposts erected, so that the market could stretch out its feelers in all directions. Napoleon, with his dead-straight, tree-lined avenues (known as *Routes Napoléon* ever since) merely extended the road network, which is still largely in use today. In an age without railways or motor cars, rivers constituted the cheapest and safest means of mass transport. Heavy and bulky articles were carried by barge, especially grain, the mainstay of the people's food supply, which had to be kept stable with the help of fixed bread prices and a smoothly running distribution. There are many navigable rivers in France, but still not enough. Consequently, Colbert organised an ingenious system of connecting canals which ensured that practically every important town in France could be reached by cargo boat. Like his road system, it is still in use today and affects the appearance of much of the French landscape. It was certainly not by chance that canals formed such an important element in the layout of the park at Versailles.

Because trade and production could not function in a vacuum, nor the free play of economic forces in a situation not yet fully developed in a capitalist sense float freely, the State stepped in almost everywhere to connect, arrange, regulate, protect or encourage what seemed at that stage progressive developments and suppressions. Many historically evolved institutions were obstructed and eventually stifled. Thus the old guilds were gradually dissolved to make way for factories with standardized quality and regulated mass production by wage labourers and skilled workers—the pattern and precondition of industrial production. Manufacture on that scale could be achieved only if a constant and uninterrupted flow of raw materials was ensured through state trading monopolies and state-controlled coal, iron and silver mines and forestry. The medieval master craftsman was superseded by a new figure: the small or big businessman and the factory owner. Where the government approved of the venture it might be encouraged by a system of tax preferences and protection, but it could also be broken by special taxation if it began to encroach on a state monopoly, because in that era of swiftly growing industry the government liked to reserve particularly lucrative branches for itself. Under the wage-earning and capitalist system old crafts swelled into wholesale manufactures: leather, glass, textiles (in France, Lyons, with practically no competition to contend with, was the centre of the silk and stocking industries), dyeing, perfumes and essences.

A protection system of state-controlled prices, protective custom-duties, the abolition of the old feudal internal duties and lords' customs privileges, and above all the institution of import duties and export bonuses, safeguarded the blossoming capitalist structure. The price of goods from abroad was artificially raised to protect the home market and production by means of custom duties, while the flow of exports was promoted by bonuses in order to maintain and increase employment in factories. Special taxes reduced the demand for articles in short supply; price reductions encouraged a quicker turnover for surplus goods. And every one of these measures brought money clinking into the state treasury.

Extremely detailed regulations regarding production, quality and preparation, the so-called *Réglements d'Etat*, ensured a constant value, and the standardized quantities and quality of certain articles. Far-reaching directional measures controlled the economy. The taxation and protection systems enabled the state to guide investment as it desired.

Without its manufacturing system the absolute State could not have achieved all its cultural projects, particularly its enormous programme of

82

Pages 79–81:
34, 35 *Versailles: Grand Trianon. Both illustrations show in detail the charm and grace of Mansart's creative gifts, which could be exercised here in a more relaxed manner than in the 'public' and ceremonial main palace of Versailles. The attractive colour scheme was entirely derived from natural rock: the flattened Ionic columns are of rose-coloured, white veined marble from Languedoc; the warm ochre limestone framing the windows came from Troissy; the quarries of the Campagna supplied the unblemished snow-white marble used for the capitals and bases of the pillars.*

palace building. The Hall of Mirrors at Versailles, for instance, an undertaking of a kind until then undreamt of in Europe, would not have been possible before the foundation of the state glassworks and mirror factories, which were at first dependent on the skill of imported Italian craftsmen. A contemporary report describes in some detail the problems that beset the infant French glass industry. In 1663 the French ambassador in Venice had managed, with great difficulty and even risk, to secure the services of a few Italian glassworkers from Murano by offering them the then fabulous wage of three to four ducats a day. They were to teach their craft to a certain number of French workers each year. In the event, however, they guarded their trade secrets jealously, for their monopoly of knowledge was their only capital. The industry, with all its expensive installation, was entirely dependent on the 'whims of foreigners'. One day an Italian foreman broke his foot. The factory had to remain idle for ten days although all the ovens were heated and the wages paid, because his French assistants were unable to take on the foreman's work and carry out a task for which he had been trained since he was twelve years old.

The hundreds of square metres of wallpaper that lined the walls of baroque palaces presuppose factory production, as do the kilometres of silk cloth for covering furniture and making curtains and wall-hangings. The furniture—hundreds of chairs, sofas, chests, writing-tables—considered essential in a baroque palace and to the new, social way of life that was led within its walls, could not have been produced without factory methods. Manufacturers also arose from the increasing expenditure of the upper classes on clothes. The growth of a 'fashion industry' in the modern sense demanded the mass production of wigs, powder, buttons, shoe buckles, belt buckles, high-heeled shoes and corsets, as well as uniforms for the various divisions of the standing army.

The growth of the war machine called for the establishment of an arms industry with fixed norms, numbers, replacements and quality. Cannon, guns, bayonets, munitions, saddles, wheels for gun-carriages and baggage wagons were made in various state and private factories. War became an industry and armaments an opportunity for profit.

The era of state-controlled economy and manufacture has rightly been called the 'age of the trade war'. It was closely connected with the foundation of the first overseas colonies as a result of the great geographical discoveries by the Spanish and Portuguese during the 16th century. It is true that wars were still waged for abstract rights and dynastic titles, but the real reasons for war were now usually disputes about overseas trade and market monopolies, sources of raw material and safe sea passages. French colonialism began 'officially' in 1603 with the appointment of Samuel de Champlain as Governor of Canada and the military occupation of Newfoundland, New Scotland and New France. Quebec was founded in 1608, Montreal in 1643. After 1625 French Jesuits were active as missionaries in south-west Canada. With the founding of the West Indian Company in 1664 the fur and spirits trade with the American Indians became a going concern. In 1674 Colbert established a special state department for the promotion of trade in the new colonial territories, and by 1690 there were 10,000 settlers in 'overseas France'. A bridgehead had been secured in the extreme south of what are now the United States as early as 1682. In the same year La Salle undertook an expedition into the Mississippi Delta, named the newly discovered land 'Louisiana' and began to establish forts. The chain of military strongpoints was completed with the founding of New Orleans in 1718.

Conflict with rival colonial powers was unavoidable. Clashes between the super-powers, England and France, were particularly frequent. The

beginnings of colonial and imperialist policies now became perceptible and
continued far into the nineteenth century. The struggle for power between
European nations in the time of Louis XIV led ultimately to the
'Europeanisation of the world', to world markets and global economic
policies, so that in the annals of the 17th and 18th centuries the names of the
heads of the East or West Indian trading companies loomed as large as those
of colonial generals. Colonial armies fought each other in distant lands, forces

36 *Versailles: Le Hameau, the Queen's House, built in 1783–1786 for the last queen of the* ancien régime, *Marie Antoinette, the wife of Louis XVI. Le Hameau stands in the grounds of Louis XV's Petit Trianon (1749–1772), not shown here. After the death of Louis XV in 1774 Louis XVI often retired to the Petit Trianon and later gave its surrounding park to Marie Antoinette as a present. The whole park was re-landscaped in the new romantic, picturesque 'English' style, inspired by the ideas of Jean-Jacques Rousseau. After 1774 the Queen's small private theatre was built there, and in 1778 the* Temple d'Amour. *Finally came a complete little artificial village with a farmhouse (*Maison de la Reine*), dairy, bridge, thatched roofs, cow stalls, servants quarters, fruit and vegetable gardens. It was an expression of the Arcadian idyll and romantic feeling for nature of the departing rococo era, with its new appreciation of free-growing, even if artificially picturesque, groups of trees, natural woodland pools, twisting paths, half-hidden ruins and romantically arranged cliffs and rocks. Here, even in 1789, the year of revolution, the last intimate little dinners enjoyed by the royal family took place.*

37 *Versailles: Le Hameau, the dairy (after 1783) – a symbol of the pretty but unpardonably frivolous, dying aristocratic world of the* ancien regime *that was taking refuge from the threatening storm clouds in an Arcadia of sentimental rusticity.*

37

38 *Versailles: The Temple of Love, lying halfway to Le Hameau (1778). This open rotunda of Corinthian columns was the prototype of whole generations of similar garden ornaments during the 18th and 19th centuries. Inside it used to stand a statue by Bouchardon (the original is now in the Louvre, a copy at Versailles) of 'Cupid cutting his bow from the club of Hercules', symbolizing the conquest of coarse physical strength by the spiritual power of feeling and love, another deliberate reference to the heroic Hercules myth of the mighty Sun King.*

38

39

partly manned by hired foreign soldiers, such as Hessian mercenaries, because the supply of coffee, tea, tobacco, raw silk, precious metal or fine timber was running short in the motherland.

The striving for world dominion by the new great powers was clearly symbolised in the art of the period. In the late 17th century and increasingly through the 18th century the interiors and gardens of palaces and great houses were characterized by exotic ornament. Chinoiserie, Turkish and Indian styles, tea pavilions, dragon motifs, Asian porcelain and silk embroideries, oriental carpets, lacquerwork, exotic plants and strange animals for the park were all the rage. The collection of objects and curiosities

39, 40 *Paris, Hotel Carnavalet: Madame de Sévigné's drawing room and blue salon. Marie de Rabutin-Chantal, Marquise de Sévigné (1626–1696), who moved in the most select circle of Louis XIV's court in Versailles, became known in literary history through her witty letters, later published, to her daughter, the Comtesse de Grignan. Like those of Liselotte von der Pfalz, they give a true and vivid picture of life at court during the* grand siècle. *She was one of the first aristocratic, clever, independent women, combining charm with intelligence and literary talent, who set the tone in 17th and 18th century society by running a literary salon. Others were the Marquise de Rambouillet (1588–1665), Madame de Scudéry (1607–1701), Ninon de Lencios (1620–1705), the Marquise de Lambert (1647–1733), the Marquise de Tencin, Madame de Geoffrin (1699–1777) and Mademoiselle de Lepinasse (1732–1776). These salons were started in the early 17th century as a form of urbane female counter-culture to the somewhat loutish landed gentry and male society at the courts of Henri IV and even Louis XIII. They soon became the meeting-place of writers, philosophers, artists and intellectual clergymen and already played a significant part as political clubs in the days of the Fronde. Finally, they developed into centres of the great literary, philosophical and scientific movements of the time. Among the frequenters of these salons, with their principles of tolerance, their strict – later too stiff and mechanical – ritual of discussion and their not only fashionable but trend-setting mannerisms of speech, were Cardinal Richelieu, La Rochefoucauld, Corneille, Molière, Fontenelle, Montesquieu, Diderot and d'Alembert. As the salons became les exclusively aristocratic they began to take a major share in disseminating the ideas that led to the revolution of 1789. The oldest part of the Hotel Carnavalet, a town house for the nobility, was built in the 16th century, but it was modernized for Madame de Sévigné from plans by Jules Hardouin-Mansart and remained her Paris home for twenty years. Today it is used as the Museum of Parisian Urban History. The Sévigné drawing-room (plate 39) is beautifully furnished in the 'royal' style of Louis XIV's reign. With its elegant pale blue panelling relieved by not over-florid white decoration, the Blue Salon (plate 40) is typical of the early rococo period (Louis Quinze).*

40

from overseas became a veritable mania. This desire for the palace to represent the whole world in miniature sprang from the political objectives of world trade and colonial expansion. That outlook was most clearly expressed in a highly fashionable subject matter for painted ceilings: the four quarters of the globe, Europe, America, Asia and Africa, a decoration no self-respecting baroque palace could afford to be without.

Agriculture remained the neglected stepchild of the state-controlled economy, threatened by cheap imports of foodstuffs from abroad, handicapped by old-fashioned farming methods and dealing more often in barter and payment in kind than in money transactions. Here, too, Colbert

stepped in. He encouraged productivity by the introduction of farm machinery, by the breeding of crops and animals that gave a better yield and by establishing experimental farms.

There can be no question but that the state-controlled economy of the *grand siècle* produced some great achievements, with results that are still perceptible to this day. But throughout the close-knit organisation the sweat of the poor was still the salt on the rich man's table, and the system of privileges, protection and tax-preferences remained unjust. The prosperous classes were helped, the exploited still further exploited. The heaviest burden of taxation fell on the small farmers, craftsmen and owners of modest businesses, thus on the poorer countryfolk and petty townsmen. The higher and lower nobility and the civil and military officers of the new State were mostly free from taxation. The rising urban middle class, on the other hand, the small factory-owners and prosperous businessmen who were so rapidly catching up socially, intellectually and economically, were, in comparison, heavily taxed. Increasingly they felt the tax and protection system that had at first opened the way for them to wealth and social influence, as an unbearable interference and a dead weight that tied them down and prevented their free upward flight to prosperity. The whirring cogwheels and jangling cash-boxes of the small urban capitalists were at last to swell into the marching tunes of

41 *Maisons Lafitte in Paris: Maisons Lafitte, a mid-17th-century creation (1642–1648) of Jules Hardouin-Manart's, was the prototype of a whole series of town or suburban residences for the French nobility active about the royal court and needing a base in the capital. It is clear that in this case Mansart was influenced by earlier examples from the 16th and early 17th centuries. Thus the high, sloping roof with its conspicuous chimneys is reminiscent of Fontainebleau and the châteaux of the Loire. The canonical order of Doric, Ionic and Corinthian columns on ground, first and top floors shows that he had studied his Serlio, Palladio or Scamozzi. However, the graceful symmetry with which the central building and two wings half embrace the forecourt, the interesting levels of the tall house with its low side-pavilions and the elegant shape of the separate parts are all his own. They set the style of Parisian town mansions during the whole 17th and 18th centuries.*

the great bourgeois revolution of 1789, when capitalism threw off its last fetter, the monarchy. For the monarchy, even in its developed form of absolutism and state-controlled economy, was still the *ancien regime* bearing the stigma of feudalism.

The German Empire

Since the later Middle Ages there had existed a latent dualism between the Holy Roman Empire (merging into the Austrian Empire) and the State, or, to be more precise, between the wearer of the imperial crown and the ruling princes of the Germanic states. The provisions of the Treaty of Westphalia (1648), guaranteed by France and Sweden, had brought that polarity to a temporary conclusion and exerted a stabilizing effect on the constitution. The princes and dignitaries of the Imperial Diet or *Reichstag*, had their full territorial sovereignty confirmed. The Empire itself became a Confederation of states with a sovereign head in the person of the emperor or *Kaiser*. The Emperor did not rule over the German people directly, but over the Imperial Diet, those who had the right to a seat and vote within it, namely the immediate rulers of the Germanic states. The frequently affirmed 'liberty' of the princes, guaranteed by France for its own purposes, included their right to contract alliances with other states, as long as they were not directed against the Emperor or the Empire. How little that proviso was respected is shewn by the French-inspired First Rhenish League of 1658 between the western and central German states. It was this right to form separate alliances that involved the single German states ever more deeply in international politics, usually to the detriment of the Empire.

The Diet, an important element in the Empire, was made up of three colleges. First, the College of the Prince Electors, with seven, later ten, votes. The Electors assembled there were assigned royal rank. Although they were seldom in total agreement with one another, they constituted the sole court empowered to elect an Emperor and they alone possessed the right to vote. With this weapon they were able to undermine the already weak position of the Emperor still further from one election to the next.

Second, under the College of Prince Electors came the College of Princes, both secular and ecclesiastical, with a hundred votes in all. Since 1641 the appointment of the princes had been dependent on the agreement of the Imperial Diet and the acquisition of noble rank.

The third College consisted of representatives of the imperial cities and were only entitled to two votes all together. They could have a say in events only after an agreed decision to that effect by both the first two colleges, which meant that they rarely played a part at all.

After the Diet had succeeded in decisively reducing the Emperor's power, the wearer of the Imperial crown, realizing his relative impotence, began to neglect the Empire in favour of his hereditary dominions and to increase the influence of his house.

Constitutionally the epoch is marked by the growing independence of the larger Germanic states, which by its end had developed into almost sovereign nations. The Empire was progressively diminished to the level of a nominal feudal overlordship with few and limited rights. As already said, the Treaty of Westphalia, an important clarification concerning the Empire and its component states, had assured the princes of their territorial sovereignty. According to the recognised legal opinion of the 18th century imperial lawyers, the Empire was a system of associated single states. For any imperial rights to be exercised on a sovereign territory required the ruler's consent. Alternately, as in Prussia, such rights were abolished altogether. By the 18th century states such as Prussia, Austria and even Hanover had effectively left the Empire. The prevailing conception of government had moved away from the medieval ideal in which the highest duty of rulers was to uphold the law and preserve peace. The idea of 'the common good' came to the fore and was not infrequently used as a justification for the violent suppression of ancient freedoms. In the approaching Age of Reason a supposedly rational system of government was invented—an ideal state on a mathematical basis (*more mathematico*) with a monarch at its apex. The absolute sovereign—in other words one free from any permanent control—felt himself to be God's representative on earth, to whom authority had been divinely granted. In the totally organized state in which the prince's will was carried out by an obedient and unquestioning officialdom the good of the people may well have been kept in mind but without allowing them any freedom or independence.

During the Age of Enlightenment that dawned during the later 18th century the religious basis of kingship fell away. Absolute monarchy developed into the absolute State, in which the prince himself appeared as merely part of the government (first servant of the State) and cast off many of his former governing functions, especially that of justice. The administration of the State became the business of the nobility, social divisions growing more pronounced than ever.

A characteristic of the old empire was the surprising variety of its component lands. They ranged from great powers, through medium states to very small ones. While the big nations were often involved in high politics, the chief concern of the little states was to preserve the *status quo*. They tended to be conservative and had some reason to fear the rationalist spirit of the time. Because of this, authority could easily deteriorate into tyranny:

'The smaller the realm, the more it depended on the personality of the Serene Highness. The minor German states of the 18th century ran through the whole gamut of possible alternatives. Patriarchal solicitude could exist side by side with an unbridled pursuit of pleasure and frivolity. The only defence was flight over the frontier, which fortunately was seldom very far away. No wonder that the ideas of the French Revolution found fertile soils in such caricatures of the police state.'

(Haller)

In spite of the political independence of the Germanic states of that period, the artistic and intellectual expressions showed so much unity of style that one forgets the fragmentation and divergence of political power.

Imperial Vienna, the capital and seat of the great Hapsburg dynasty, held a special place within the European framework. Even though the Electors, as leading powers in the Empire, sought selfishly to promote their own dynastic importance, often at the Empire's cost, they did not entirely disregard Viennese policy. The unbroken links between the German princes and the court of Vienna explain the strong influence of Viennese architecture on neighbouring south Germany. The art of building in the capital during the decade following the Thirty Years War was almost entirely of Italian origin. The 'Am Hof' square, new Forum Sacrum of Vienna, the Leopoldinian wing of the Hofburg palace, and the Herrenstadt with its great palaces of the nobility were almost without exception designed and built by Italian architects. The most important 17th century ecclesiastical building in Vienna, the façade of the Jesuit Church (1662), is also the work of an Italian master builder, Carlo Antonio Carlone. However, in the last decade of the 17th century Italy's dominant influence on the art and architecture of the imperial city was checked by two German artists, the master builders Johann Bernhard Fischer von Erlach (1656–1723) and Johann Lucas von Hildebrandt (1668–1745). Their architectural works, designed soon after the victory over the Turks,

42 *Vienna, the Upper Belvedere: the wrought iron gates in front of the forecourt. The triple entrance with its commanding central gates marks the boundary of the palace gardens and so divides the park area from the unregimented open ground outside. The centre portal, still further dignified by the imperial arms on the supporting pillars, is in direct line with the middle point of the palace façade. The wrought iron gates made by Arnold Küffner in 1728 bear witness to the expert craftsmanship and high artistic level of the time that imprinted their style and shape on every material used. Although the two side gates are made of ordinary cast iron, one feels that in the crowning top section of the portal the technical and aesthetic potentialities of iron-working have been extended to the frontiers of the possible.*

43

43 *Vienna, Upper Belvedere: the Court of Honour (1720–1724) seen from the front. The palace frontage facing the entrance gates is characterized by the extensive width of its various sections, all cohesively held together by the lively, flowing contours of the roof. By* *avoiding all the architectural clichés of the day and deliberately aiming for a theatrical effect, Hildebrandt, the architect, achieved a work of great individuality. He constructed a large basin extending along the whole frontage to produce the illusion of a floating palace.*

have left their indelible stamp on the era. Emperor Leopold and Prince Eugene, the most eminent political personalities of that time, whose names are indissolubly linked with the final driving back of the Turkish threat, discovered in von Erlach and Hildebrandt artists after their own hearts. In the two outstanding Viennese palaces, Schönbrunn and the Belvedere, the architects created seminal works of art that expressed the heroic self-confidence of the epoch.

Fischer's career in Vienna began in the 'eighties. His first authenticated work there was the Grabensäule, which he designed in collaboration with the best known court artists. His first architectural commission came from Prince Franz Adam zu Lichtenstein, who asked him to build the Belvedere palace in the grounds of Rossau. It is no chance that a member of that family should have opened the way for Fischer. Lichtenstein saw the creation of noble architecture as a princely obligation, and told his son and heir that 'only the splendid buildings left behind by a dynasty will keep its memory green', which sheds a clear light on the motivation behind the princely palace-builders of the baroque age.

44

44   *Vienna, the Upper and Lower Belvederes. The palace grounds, lying south of the old town, outside the ring of fortified city walls, were originally in the unbuilt-up approaches to the capital. The extensive town building that has taken place in the 19th and 20th centuries has destroyed the uninterrupted merging of the open parkland into the heart of the city and so robbed it of much of its effect. Nevertheless, the masterly lay-out of the two axially related palaces with their lawns and avenues is* *sufficiently isolated by well proportioned gardens and open ground for the original conception to be still clearly recognisable, in spite of the very different style of the circumambient housing. Schwarzenburg Palace, seen above on the right of the Belvedere, is another of the summer palaces and parks that arose after the Turkish menace had been repelled and it was possible to site them outside the city walls that protected the old part of the town.*

45 *Vienna, the Upper Belvedere; outside the Grand entrance hall as seen from the forecourt. The upper palace, designed by Lukas von Hildebrandt, and built between 1720 and 1724, was the final and crowning work in the whole architectural and horticultural complex of the Belvedere.*

Indicative of Fischer's rise to the high position at court formerly reserved for Italians was his appointment as teacher to the Crown Prince Joseph in 1689. His task was 'to instruct His Royal Highness in architecture, perspective and related sciences . . . for one hour every day . . .', an illustration of the degree to which the practice and theory of architecture and allied subjects were taken for granted as a necessary part of an aristocrat's education.

The Crown Prince's architect was granted the honourable and influential rank of Royal Architect-in-Chief. Not the least of its advantages was that it strengthened the position of the 'German party' at court in its resistance to the 'cultural imperialism' of France. The political power struggle between France and the House of Hapsburg was accompanied by cultural disagreements, of which Hans Jacob Wagner von Wagenbach, author of *Ehrenruff Teutschlands*, was the spokesman. The author, who taught the Crown Prince history, opposed all foreign influence, and never tired of telling his imperial pupil his two maxims: not to trust foreigners, and not to prefer foreigners to his own countrymen. That ideology suited the new court architect very well.

Fischer passed his first test with flying colours on the occasion of the coronation of Joseph I as King of Rome in Augsburg (1690). For the ceremonial procession in Vienna Fischer designed two triumphal arches which showed his versatile gifts as both architect and decorator in a most favourable light. That was enough to send the patriotic xenophobe, Wagenbach, into wordy raptures on the superiority of German art to any trumpery from over the border. He ended with the words:

'And this was a glorious day of triumph and honour, on which not only did Your Royal Majesty ride resplendent through the world-dominating city of Vienna like an angel sent from Heaven for the happiness of his people, in incomparable splendour perfectly ordered by German ingenuity, but on which German art and skill also won a notable victory over the adulation of foreigners in the hearts of all the spectators.'

After 1690 the political purpose that Fischer's art was to play at the Viennese court became increasingly plain. Soon after the coronation of the twelve-year-old Crown Prince as King of Rome, the idea of a German Versailles began to germinate in the minds of the patriotic German teacher and his circle. The plan arose naturally from the emblematic decorations on the triumphal arches. On one of the arches the young king was shewn sitting enthroned before the solar disc, dispensing light; on the other he drove the sun horses of Helios four-in-hand. So it is not surprising that the German Sun King needed a German Versailles, especially since the rival palace outside the gates of Paris was also permeated with allegorical sun symbols: Versailles, where the life-giving Sun, Louis XIV, rested in the garden of the Hesperides after his labours.

The self-esteem of the Hapsburg realm, fortified by victory over the Turks, now craved for some tangible architectural expression to proclaim the might and renown of the Holy Roman Emperors, as well as to see the French, who, as quasi-allies of the Turks, were already discomfited on the field of battle, defeated again in the field of artistic endeavour. So the artist Fischer von Erlach was assigned the task of demonstrating the ascendancy of the German emperors by building a palace, the seat of the true Sun King, which would eclipse the world-renowned palace of Versailles.

The first design for this super-Versailles was prepared as early as 1690. In this monumental but never realized project the Schönbrunn Palace was to have crowned the eminence now occupied by the 'Gloriette', the memorial to the victory at Kolin. The architect had a twofold assignment: to beat the

Pages 96–97:

46 *Vienna, Upper Belvedere: the garden room. This room, decorated with paintings by Gaetano Fantis, lies in the central part of the building and is a halfway house between the interior and the meticulously proportioned gardens. The fantastic architectural scenes created by the illusional painting show a typical pageant of baroque allegory, the central figures, Apollo and Aurora, representing light defeating darkness. The subject symbolizes Prince Eugene's victory over the Turks.*

47 *Vienna, Upper Belvedere: the Marble Hall, named after its predominant material. This sumptuous apartment is the central room of the palace. Italian artists were specially imported by the architect to paint the walls and ceiling. The colour harmony of the red marble with the greenish murals and gold capitals gives the room its special richness. Formal magnificence, attained by a mixture of real and painted architecture in the high baroque style, is the room's keynote. Slanted*

corners transform its shape into an octagon, the lower part of the walls cleanly and austerely articulated by double pillars. A wide, richly-framed cornice runs between this area and the vaulted ceiling, which is made to look even higher than it really is by its perspectives of painted architecture.

48 *Vienna, Upper Belvedere: the main staircase, From a half-way landing two simple, graceful outer flights rise to the passage in front of the Marble Hall, while a central stairway leads down to the Garden Room. The whole staircase and well, including the delicate plasterwork carried out by Santino Bossi between 1722 and 1723, are snow-white, forming a neutral transition between the colourful Marble Hall and the rest of the palace.*

French at their own game of palace-building and at the same time put the second artistic hegemony, Italy, in the shade. In attempting that task, however, he made use of the artistic repertory of the very French and Italian cultures he was aiming to supersede. Fischer von Erlach combined the ground-plan of Versailles with the classic order of columns Bernini had designed for the never completed façade of the Louvre, and used a Perrault-style temple frontage as a main theme of the Könisburg, adding a pediment that gave it the look of a sacred edifice. The superiority to Versailles of this projected palace complex lay mostly in its situation. It was to stand on high ground, overlooking the 'limitless town of Vienna as far as eye can see, and to the Hungarian border' (Fischer von Erlach). Thus the palace was related on one side to Vienna, the imperial capital, and on the other to the frontier of Hungary, whose king lived in the palace, elevated to a symbol of world dominion. Echoing the sun symbolism of Versailles, a gigantic quadriga drawing the chariot of Apollo-Joseph crowned the centre of the building and united the whole complex in a system of allegory symbolizing the virtues of the sovereign. It included the Hercules emblems in the entrance area and extended to the statues in the water garden depicting Apollo killing the python and Hercules overpowering Cerberus. In the language of baroque iconography they were both meant to symbolize the strength of the ruler in overcoming the powers of darkness.

The huge project was never carried out, because, as a result of the long wars, the imperial treasury could not afford it. Nevertheless, to judge by the plans, accompanied by the series of engravings in Fischer's famous *Historical Architecture*, the artistic intentions and the allegorically represented political pretensions of the period were more clearly expressed in this project than in any actual later building.

Had the first Schönbrunn plans been put into effect, the Emperor and Empire would have achieved an architectural exaltation of their political power unsurpassed in the whole of Europe. Be that as it may, the unrealized plans served as a basis and inspiration for numerous princely residences throughout the Empire, so that Fischer's perfected synthesis of French and Italian styles proved an extraordinarily fruitful influence on German baroque buildings. His architectural ideas, spreading out from Austria, determined the style of building in all the neighbouring regions and states: Hungary, Bohemia, Silesia and Saxony, Poland, Franconia and areas bordering the Middle and Upper Rhine. German master builders, including Neumann, Pöppelmann, Welsch and others, made their pilgrimage to Vienna, glittering stage of the theatre of architecture. For them Vienna took the place of Rome, whose buildings had been the centre of attraction and an object of study to earlier generations of architects.

In the rest of the Empire the style of the first Schönbrunn project was adopted by those princes whose feelings of belonging to the Empire had been strengthened by the Turkish wars, among them the Margrave Ludwig von Baden, vanquisher of Turks, and the extensive family of Schönborn, who held so many of the secular and ecclesiastical offices of the Empire. Feeling, as they did, separate if not actively hostile to the Empire, Bavaria and later Prussia kept outside the fashionable movement and modelled themselves on other political and artistic examples. In accordance with his political leaning towards France, on whose side he had entered the field against the Empire in the War of the Spanish Succession, the Bavarian Elector's great palaces of Nymphenburg and Schleissheim near Munich were clearly built under French influence.

More difficult to assess are the influences that affected the state buildings of Augustus the Strong. The royal orangery in Dresden—better known as the

49 *Vienna, Schönbrunn Palace: general view of the park and the garden front of the palace. In the foreground the 'Gloriette', the victory memorial for the battle of Kolin, 1757. The palace was begun in 1696 from plans made by Bernhard Fischer von Erlach, the Court Architect, in 1693. By 1732 the building was virtually completed. Only a few years later, in 1744, the palace was considerably rebuilt and altered both inside and out. The baroque addiction to axiality decided the arrangement of buildings and park. The latter is laid out in the French style with symmetrical lawns divided by wide avenues leading in a straight line to the palace. The horizontal mass of the main building is to some extent balanced by the Gloriette memorial, a long, arcaded structure standing on higher ground.*

Zwinger—was the architectural setting for many of that brilliant monarch's magnificent entertainments. In the opinion of the German art historian George Dehio, no other building of the century displayed so much charming originality. The uniqueness of the creation comes from the variety of its sources of inspiration. One is the design by the Viennese architect Lukas von Hildebrandt for a garden and orangery for the Schönborn Palace in Vienna, while the ground plan shows some resemblance to that of the Rastatt palace.

The whole spectrum of European artistic influences in the baroque age can be traced in the palace-building of the Elector Palatine, Johann Wilhelm von der Pfalz (1658–1716), who brought artists from all over Europe to his court at Düsseldorf. A typical example of this pan-European architectural style can be seen in the palatial hunting lodge built for him by the ennobled Venetian architect, Count Matteo Alberti (1647–1735) at Bensberg near Cologne. It was constructed round a main courtyard and finished in 1710. In this work Alberti, who had been active as an engineer in Paris between 1672 and 1682, was inspired not only by the dazzling example of Versailles, but even more by ideas from England. In London in 1683 he had met Sir Christopher Wren, the most important English architect of the age. Hampton Court Palace and the never-completed palace at Winchester exercised a lasting fascination on the Venetian master. The impressions he received in England were developed into a very personal creation when he designed the Bensberg Schloss, although he never denied the source of his inspiration. The English influence was also partly due to the Elector's friendship with the Duke of Marlborough, who was his guest at Bensberg in 1705 and was received in a magnificent tent, because the palace itself was not yet habitable.

German rulers in favour of religious tolerance gained great benefits for their countries from the settlement there of Huguenot refugees who had been driven from their homes by the Edict of Nantes in 1685. Most of the refugees came from the educated classes and had a distinctly advantageous effect on the artistic and economic life of their host countries, especially in regard to urban and residential architecture. A family of architects and builders called Du Ry gave the town of Cassel, residence of the prince, an irreplaceable character, most of which was lost in a bomb attack on October 22nd 1943.

Politically and culturally Brandenburg was in rather a special situation. During the Thirty Years War it had been devastated and depopulated, but under the rule of Friedrich Wilhelm, the Great Elector (1640–1688), it had blossomed anew into an economically flourishing and politically and militarily respected state. The young prince had been deeply impressed by the northern Netherlands, whither he had travelled to meet his first wife, a daughter of the Prince of Orange-Nassau. After living in Cleves on the lower Rhine until 1650 he moved to Berlin and later resided in Potsdam. He built extravagantly furnished palaces with extensive parks one of them being Oranienburg. This royal residence betrayed a definitely Dutch influence, no doubt in honour of his queen, Louise Henriette's, homeland. The Great Elector's favourite residence was his Potsdam town seat, begun in 1679, which was also Dutch in its general layout. Several times renovated and altered by his successors, it was considered one of the finest examples of Brandenburg–Prussian architecture until it was demolished in 1959 after being burnt out fourteen years earlier. Friedrich Wilhelm I built several other palaces fo purposes of display and improved the already existing palace in Berlin. To help him carry out his building projects he employed Andreas Schlüter, master builder, sculptor and decorator, a superlative artist. This architect not only gave the Berlin palace its ultimate form, a unique masterpiece among German baroque palaces, but also originated a 'Prussian style in which the emotional force of the Baroque (the spirit of Bernini, perhaps), blended with the rational, classical monumentality of a Perrault or Mansart, was elevated to a composite but balanced, restrained and noble form.' (E. Berckenhagen)

50 *Vienna, Schönbrunn Palace: the north façade facing the forecourt and great fountain. The illustration gives a good idea of Fischer's design, with the row of half-columns, the elevated attic storey and the sweeping outer staircase of the middle portion connected to the two wings by equally large intermediate sections. The whole composition gains unity and strength from the vertical lines of the columns and the horizontal window rows of the two upper storeys. A rusticated ground floor supports the series of columns.*

51 *Vienna, Schönbrunn Palace: view of the park and Gloriette. The garden façade of the palace looks on to a strictly symmetrical garden in the French style, with a central avenue ending at the tree-encircled Neptune Fountain. From there the ground slopes gently upwards under velvety grass to the open arcades of the Gloriette, which gives the eye a resting point in the surrounding open space. Its pavilion-like architecture is related to that of Prince Eugene's Belvederes.*

52 *Vienna, Schönbrunn Palace: a wing seen from the garden side. In addition to the broad central pathway at right angles to the palace façade (plate 49), there are converging avenues that afford enchanting oblique glimpses of the building. The artistic juxtaposition of pool, avenue and almost casual view of the palace gives the vista its special charm.*

England

While the Thirty Years War was raging on the continent, England was too much concerned with her own internal politics to involve herself with hostilities abroad. Her trading and sea power had emerged strengthened from the war with Spain. The nation could now turn its attention to colonisation overseas and an expansion of the merchant and fighting fleets. That brought England up against the colonial and naval power of Holland, who, after initial victories at sea finally succumbed to English naval superiority. The most important result of that conflict was the Navigation Act of 1651, to which defeated Holland was forced to consent. Thenceforth colonial merchandise might be carried only in English ships, while goods from the continent had to be transported either in English vessels or in those belonging to the country of origin. This transport monopoly could be put into practice through English successes at sea, so that the merchant fleet of Holland, the 'carrier of Europe', was effectively outmanoeuvred.

While power politics in England at that time might be pursued with pragmatic astuteness, they were not necessarily mixed up with national feeling. Not many years later, in 1688, the same Englishmen chose the protestant figurehead of the Netherlands freedom movement, William of Orange, to be their king. 'For the Protestant religion and a free parliament against the Stuarts and Catholic restoration' was their slogan, for it was known that the Stuarts favoured Catholicism and wanted to establish an absolute monarchy after the French pattern.

With a representative of the fight for Protestantism and freedom seated on the throne, albeit with his authority was severely limited by the Bill of Rights, the island state felt ready to face Louis XIV's pretensions to hegemony. A change of allegiance had already occurred during the war between France and Holland. At first an ally of the French, England eventually joined the Emperor in coming to the aid of the Dutch. The explanation of the change lies in the political principle regarding the command of the English Channel, which England felt to be threatened by a French occupation of Holland. When William of Orange ascended the English throne the opposition hardened. Skilled in diplomacy, he organized the so-called Grand Alliance against the might of France, in which the Austrian Emperor, Spain, Sweden, Brandenburg, Saxony, Hanover, Savoy, England and Holland were all united. It was too much for Louis XIV. By the Peace of Ryswijk he was forced to relinquish his conquests. The zenith of France's power was over.

Tension between outmanoeuvred France and the pan-European coalition came to a head in 1701, when the last Spanish Hapsburg died without an heir. One of the claimants to the vacant throne was the Austrian Hapsburg, the Archduke Charles, who considered himself the best qualified pretender by virtue of the so-called Second Succession. On the other hand, it was claimed that a disputed clause in the will of the late Spanish king had bequeathed his throne to Philip, a grandson of Louis XIV, although with the reservation that the two lands of Spain and France should never be united. At the court of Versailles, where this last proviso was suppressed, the news caused great rejoicing and cries of 'The Pyrenees are no more!'

The threatened union of the two nations into one great power raised fierce opposition from England, which, since 1689, and after her experience of France's appetite for expansion, had become the enthusiastic champion of an European balance of power. Once again she urged an alliance of European states against France. In three great battles the French army was decisively defeated by the coalition forces under the Duke of Marlborough and Prince Eugene. That was the end of the French dream of predominance in Europe.

53 Schönbrunn Palace: partial view of the Neptune Fountain. This magnificent fountain, completed in 1780, is the terminus and focal point of the garden's main axis. Cascades stream into the basin over a high stone plinth. Above it, surmounting a pyramidal rock formation pierced by a grotto, stands the sea god Neptune in commanding pose, flanked by his court of naiads and tritons.

54 *Potsdam, the palace of Sansouci Garden frontage. From a rough sketch drawn with Frederick the Great's own hand in 1774, the king's architect, George Wenzel von Knobelsdorff, built the summer palace of Sanssouci (1745–1747) that was to become the Prussian monarch's favourite seat. The king expected his ground plan and certain details of the interior and the decoration to be accurately followed. His ideas, which laid great stress on comfort and convenience, naturally came into collision with the artistic views of the equally stubborn architect. Among oher things, Frederick wanted the single-storey building to open out on to as wide a promenade as possible. Knobelsdorff, on the other hand, wished the frontage to be built near the edge of the terrace so that the palace would look well from afar. The king won, of course. He gained a spacious promenade, but at the price of spoiling the more distant view of the palace. Seen from the foot of the six orangery terraces, the palace appears to be half sunk into the ground, cut off from view by the upper terrace. Along the single-storeyed façade tall, arched windows allowing free access to the open air alternate with double columns surmounted by gusts of satyrs and bacchantes. The oval apartment in the middle is crowned with a dome. The french windows were made to the king's order, as were also the three easy steps in place of the usual podium. In fact, everything was planned to suit Frederick's personal life style, and Sanssouci was one of the few baroque palaces to lack the grand staircase considered so essential to baroque ceremonial. Whereas in other palaces the splendid state apartments were uninhabitable, his oval Marble Room at Sanssouci was almost cosy. There, when weather permitted, he entertained the most distinguished intellects of the day at his famous round table. Of these meetings of the wise and witty Voltaire wrote, 'At no other court in the world do men speak so freely of all kinds of human superstition, nowhere are these treated with so much mockery and contempt as at the suppers of the King of Prussia. God is respected, but those who cheat men in His name are not spared'.*

France was also defeated by England at sea and in the colonies. The Treaty of Utrecht in 1713 handed over to Great Britain the island of Newfoundland, Acadia and the territory round Hudson Bay. She also obtained possession of Gibraltar and Minorca, thereby gaining a decisive influence in the Mediterranean and a stage on the passage to India.

English internal politics in the first half of the 17th century were dominated by the struggle between the King, with an eye to absolutism in the French style, on the one side, and a large part of the nobility together with an independent middle class on the other. James I (1603–1625), highly educated for a sovereign of his time, was obsessed by theories of divine right, according to which God appointed kings, and kings were answerable for their actions to God alone. His subjects owed him perfect obedience. In the matter of the English constitution and national institutions James also held that parliament exercised a purely advisory function and that the common law courts were only for 'everyday' jurisdiction. In case of need he thought a king was empowered to override acts of parliament or the law's decisions. A royal council and royal law courts should take over their authority. The power of the court of Star Chamber, an institution already active under the Tudors as an agent of the royal will, was increased.

Opposition came mainly from the propertied classes: the noble owners of great estates, the landed gentry and the upper middle classes engaged in trade and finance. The heart of the dispute was consent to taxation, which lay with parliament. They took the legal standpoint that 'the king had to support himself' by drawing his income for running the country from royal possessions or, at any rate, from royal taxes. Only in special emergencies would Parliament be prepared to allow the necessary funds to be obtained by taxation. Moreover, Parliament sought, by strengthening the legislature, to protect the personal freedom, life and property of all subjects against forcible encroachment by the sovereign. During James I's reign the struggle for emancipation was frustrated by religious controversy between different parliamentary groups, so that there was no open breach with the king. When his successor, Charles I, inherited the crown in 1625, however, things came to a head. The new king favoured the Catholics and aspired to an absolute monarchy. When Parliament refused to sanction the taxation he demanded, Charles obtained the necessary income by means of forced loans and other illegal measures. In the end he ruled for ten years without a parliament. The hour for parliamentary resistance struck when the Presbyterian Scots rebelled against a proposed expansion of the Anglican Church into their country and invaded England. The king, having no money to muster an army, was forced to turn to Parliament for special taxation. Charles had to pay a heavy price: dismissal of his chief adviser, abolition of the royal jurisdiction and repeal of illegal taxation—those taxes not authorized by Parliament. The most important political factor that emerged from the seven-year Civil War was a disciplined professional army. Its organiser and commander was Oliver Cromwell, who with his officers 'purged' Parliament. What was left—the Rump Parliament—consisted of Cromwell's supporters who, in the end, ordered the king's execution.

At first Cromwell advocated strong parliamentary rule. Later, dissatisfied with the Rump Parliament as representatives of the people, he dissolved it and thereafter ruled with dictatorial sternness, supported by the army. This form of government was based on the strong will and personality of Cromwell himself, and did not survive his death. Attempts to turn the kingdom into a republic failed and the monarchy was restored. In 1660 Parliament invited the son of the beheaded king to return from his exile in France. He ascended the throne as Charles II, but only on condition that he ruled in collaboration with

55   *Dresden, the Zwinger: the* Glockenspiel-pavillon *(the pavilion of Chimes). Augustus the Strong, King of Poland and Elector of Saxony, commissioned his Architect Royal, Matthäus Daniel Pöppelmann (1662–1723), to build him a suite of pavilions, inter-connected to form a quasi-horseshoe shape, as an annexe to the old and nearly square Dresden Palace. The pavilions, which were more or less completed between 1711 and 1723, were to fulfil two separate functions, one of which emerged only in the course of building. Originally it was to have been an orangery to house precious Mediterranean plants during the winter. The second purpose soon arose, namely to act as Assembly Rooms* for grand court festivities to the glory of the absolute monarchy. The trial run for the Zwinger as a setting for parties was the celebration of the wedding between the Elector's heir and Maria Josepha, daughter of the Emperor. That by no means exhausted the possibilities of the versatile structure. On the King's written order, the royal library and other effects were transferred to the Zwinger in 1728. Gradually, the building became a veritable museum with public art galleries. A 'director general' had been installed as early as 1720. That the orangery, or rather green-house, developed into the 'Palais Royal des Sciences' illustrates the amazing and ul-timately lasting career of the original pleasure *palace. Moreover, the building in itself is an unrivalled example of Saxon baroque archi-tecture, not least because the architect, Pöppelmann, found in Balthasar Permoser (1651–1732) a congenial sculptor who contri-buted greatly to the beauty of the Zwinger.*

56 Melk Abbey on the Danube. The dignitaries of the Church in the baroque era were no less desirous of display and artistic perfection for their ecclesiastical buildings than the princes of this world for their palaces. And no ecclesiastical building of the 18th century better represents the high baroque style than the Benedictine monastery of Melk, high above the Danube. After the devastating fire of 1683 the abbot, Berthold Dietmayr, gave orders for the monastery and abbey to be completely rebuilt by the master builder Jakob Prandtauer (1660–1726). Work started in 1702. An unusual feature of the extensive building area was that it contained both monastery and princely residence, a complete break with the existing tradition of monastic organisation. Melk was not alone in this, however. Gottweig and Klosterneuburg in Austria and Banz in Germany followed the same trend, and there were others outside the German-speaking world. The vast and splendid Escorial, situated in a dominating position above Madrid, is royal palace, church and monks' living quarters in one. It was a new type of monastery that came to be regarded as the ideal plan for churches in many parts of Europe during the 18th century. The most remarkable thing about Prandtauer's artistic achievement is the way he adapted the abbey buildings to the existing land formation. The widely triangular complex is built on a trapezoidal ridge of rock, the most important parts, church, library and state apartments, looking steeply down to the Danube from a jutting crag. Rising between the two impressive wings formed by the library and imperial hall of state is the twin-towered abbey church. In front of it is a horseshoe-shaped terrace, a sort of court of honour, situated on the very edge of the dizzying cliff above the river.

a parliament. After the chaos of the Civil War and the austere rule of Oliver Cromwell it was not difficult for the new king, a wily diplomat, to present himself as the guarantor of internal peace. He was able to avoid too much conflict with his parliaments over tax questions, because his exchequer was covertly replenished by money from his cousin, the King of France, payment for his compliance with French foreign policy.

Although Charles was probably a secret Catholic, he made no open attempt to turn the country into an absolutist Catholic state, especially as the Church of England had an equally stabilizing effect on government. He made skilful use of the political and religious divisions in the land, and by playing one against the other gradually increased the power of the Crown until at his death in 1685 he was well on the way to absolute monarchy. His brother and successor, James II, a very different man, soon lost all the power Charles had gained. He was a convinced Catholic and his dearest wish was to restore the former religion to England. He could not have chosen a worse moment. The latent anti-Catholicism which his brother had kept so tactfully under control flared up as a result of the persecution of the Huguenots in France. In spite of opposition by politically aware elements all over the country, James would not retreat one step in his efforts to Romanize the kingdom. When hopes that he would be succeeded by his Protestant daughters, Mary and Anne, were dashed by the birth of a son and heir to his second wife, Parliament called on William of Orange, Stadholder of Holland, husband and cousin of Mary, to come to England, drive out his father-in-law and at least temporarily accept the crown. Abandoned by both army and navy, James fled to France after what became known as the Glorious Revolution. His dream of winning back the throne with the help of French gold and Irish Catholic troops was finally shattered at the Battle of the Boyne in 1690. That was the end of all attempts at absolute monarchy in England. She became a constitutional monarchy with a representative government and an hereditary but effectively limited royal executive. The constitutional agreement on the limited authority of the king and the sovereignty of Parliament was laid down in the Bill of Rights and recognised by the Dutch prince who became William III of England. The Bill of Rights was made law by act of Parliament. Its provisions stipulated that Catholics would be excluded from the succession, while the king might not interfere with the course of justice, impose taxation without consent of Parliament or maintain a standing army. The rights of citizens were confirmed and Parliamentary freedom of assembly and speech guaranteed.

The introduction of a constitutional monarchy (not yet a democracy in the modern sense, but an oligarchy of the propertied classes) had important consequences for the country's cultural development. England did not have the political and psychological conditions conducive to the building of baroque palaces, the expression of continental absolutism. Certainly the English sovereigns still possessed a number of castles and palaces built in medieval or Tudor times, which they subsequently enlarged and modernised, but a Versailles, dream of every petty German prince, was denied them. They continued to live in the fine old palaces of Whitehall, St James and Hampton Court as well as at Windsor Castle, originally built by William the Conqueror.

The English aristocracy, on the other hand, sometimes commissioned great country houses similar in style to contemporary palaces on the continent. An example is the Duke of Marlborough, the greatest general of his day and a distinguished diplomat. He was voted a large sum of money by Parliament and spent it on building the magnificent Blenheim Palace, named after his victory at Blenheim (Blindheim near Hochstadt on the Danube). It was designed by John Vanbrugh who, if not the most important English architect

of the time, was certainly the boldest and most individual. Under his direction there arose a building that can be seen as England's answer to the challenge of the European baroque palace. It aimed almost entirely at grandeur and display. Blenheim's superb exterior and elegant interior can more than bear comparison with its counterparts on the mainland.

Russia

The Russian nation owes its origin to penetration in the 9th century by Swedish invaders known as Varangians. The union of Varangian dominions that developed did not include the region of 'the Occident' as it was called in the Middle Ages. That area lay under the artistic and political influence of Roman Byzantium. Conversion to the Greek Orthodox Church in 1000 A.D. and growing economic and cultural contact with Constantinople had a definitive effect on the evolution of the Russian states, which were sharply segregated from the rest of Europe. In the 13th century they were conquered by the Tartar hordes led by Genghis Khan. Under this Mongolian rule, which lasted until the end of the 15th century, Russia was completely cut off from western influences.

Then one of the subject Russian states, the Archduchy of Moscow, began to stand out from the rest. Through military successes over the Tartars, Moscow became the nucleus of a growing Russian nation into which the smaller states were absorbed. When Ivan III conquered Novgorod in 1480, and then part of the Ukraine, he laid the foundations of an expanding Russian empire, a policy he underlined by adopting the title of Emperor derived from the now defunct Byzantine Empire.

Ivan the Terrible (1553–1584) followed the same policy by conquering Astrakhan and Kazan. Expeditions, partly mercantile and partly military, penetrated into Siberia. At the same time contact was made with western Europe, assuming concrete form in trade agreements with England. The Romanovs, who reigned after 1613, pursued the same line. The most forceful ruler of that dynasty, Peter the Great (1689–1725), finally elevated Russia to the rank of a Great Power. His ambition was to re-form his country to a European model and gain for her access to the seas. The latter aspiration required expansion in two directions. His advance towards the south inevitably meant collision with the powerful Turkish Empire and led to protracted hostilities dogged by fluctuating fortunes but ending in the capture of Asov on the Black Sea. The second thrust was to the Baltic coast, an enterprise that was to bring Russia in closer contact with western Europe. Meanwhile reforms in old Russia were ruthlessly pursued. An army trained by European methods, the building of a fleet, improvement of handicrafts, trade and administration were the measures by which the ambitious ruler planned to bring his people up to the admired European standards in quick tempo.

Penetration to the Baltic Sea led to conflict with Sweden, who, since the Treaty of Westphalia in 1648 had incorporated the Baltic states of Livonia, Estonia and Ingermanland into her state system. In his campaign to win a port on the ice-free Baltic coast Peter the Great was joined by two allies, Augustus of Saxony and Poland, and the Danish king. During the Northern War that started in 1700 Charles XII of Sweden first defeated the Russians at Narva, then, underrating his Russian adversary, turned against Augustus the Strong, conquered Poland and forced Augustus to abdicate. Meanwhile Peter the Great, having radically reformed his army, took over Sweden's possessions on the Baltic Sea, and at last utterly defeated Charles XII in 1709 at Poltava in the Ukraine. In 1721 the Peace of Nysted conclusively broke

Sweden's predominance in the Baltic. Livonia, Estonia, the mouth of the Neva and a part of Karelia fell into Russian hands. With the conquest of these coastal areas Russia was able to prepare her position as a Great Power in the Baltic Sea.

Even while Charles XII was invading Poland in 1703 Peter the Great was embarking on a plan to build a new city on the swampy, almost inaccessible delta of the Neva that would serve his political, military and commercial aims. The first move was to construct the Peter-and-Paul Fortress on an island to form the starting point of the future town. Its position on the Neva and close to the Gulf of Finland ensured its access to the then very important inland trading area of the Baltic.

St Petersburg owed nothing to traditional Russian town planning. It absorbed on a huge scale every idea that had been dreamt of in the urban architecture of western Europe but never fully realized. No wonder, then, that up to the middle of the 19th century the urban planners and architects of Europe were eager to leave their mark on the new capital. There they found a field of endeavour that for scope and potentiality had not its like in all western Europe.

From town plans drawn up at the beginning of the 18th century one can form a good idea of the general shape, position and extent of St Petersburg (now Leningrad) in its early days. Where the Neva river is at its widest the Peter-and-Paul Fortress designed by the Italian Domenico Trezzini, stands just in front of the St Petersburg island, which was already traversed for most of its length by two street systems.

The topography of the town is unusual. In the neighbourhood of the fortress and the St Petersburg island—thus where mainland and island are very close to one another—the housing became denser, forming a town centre. The different parts of the town are divided by the Neva, and its great width demanded a certain uniformity of architecture on a grand scale, regardless of detail, to preserve coherence of design over great stretches of water.

In 1716 the architect Leblond (1679–1719), a pupil of the garden designer Le Nôtre, came to St Petersburg. As 'Architect General' he was put in charge of all building projects in the rapidly growing city. In 1717 he produced a general conceptual outline for the whole town. In this the ground plan was an ellipse in which the heart of the town was situated in the centre of Wassily Island and co-ordinated with the St Petersburg side and the left bank of the Neva. In the heart of the town Leblond, borrowing from Italian sources, sited the Tzar's palace in the middle of a huge square. From there avenues radiated in various directions, interrupted at intervals along their course by more squares. Leblond's ideal town was bounded and circumscribed by a system of fortifications. However, the arrangement of the town that was already built prevented Leblond's plans from being properly carried out. The military protection of the town and the mouth of the Neva was already assured by the maritime fort of Kronstadt to seaward, rendering superfluous the ring of fortifications, which would in any case have hindered the growth of the town.

As already said, building operations began on Wassily Island in 1703. In 1704 work was started on the Admiralty complex; by 1707 the first part of the Alexander Nevsky Monastery was ready as well as the town's main thoroughfare, the Nevsky Prospect. At first the buildings seem to have been distributed haphazardly along the banks of the Neva. It was not till the early 19th century that the last vacant sites were built on. The Russian capital at las assumed the form conceived in the first architectural plans of Peter the Great's reign.

Pages 114–115:

57 *Melk Abbey: the library. In conformity with the traditions of the Benedictine order, which had been relatively unaffected by the medieval reforms and adhered to the prime importance of learning and the care of ancient documents, the library (1729–1731) of Melk Abbey was furnished with a lavish splendour that could bear comparison with any royal library of its day. The lofty walls are lined with two architecturally framed storeys of bookshelves. A gallery running between the two storeys makes it possible to reach the upper shelves, which rise up to the cornice of a vaulted ceiling painted to resemble open sky swarming with angelic figures. The subject of this allegorical painting, executed by Paul Tröger between 1731 and 1732, is 'Divine Wisdom and her Virtues'.*

58 *Melk Abbey: the Marble Hall. The state hall, adjoining the library end of equal size, forms the extremity of the monastic or south wing. Red marble columns run from floor to cornice, single along the short sides of the room, double on the longer sides, with atlantes supporting the capitals. The cove vaulting is decorated with illusionist architectural painting continuing the actual architecture of the room. The ceiling itself is decorated with a fine fresco (1731), also by Paul Tröger. An ideal celestial realm is filled with flying figures representing 'The Triumph of Temperance' illustrated by 'Hercules, the Conqueror of Vice'.*

116

Important Baroque Palaces

Versailles

The Palace

No one of rank and education living in the late 17th century or at any time in the 18th would have raised any serious objection if Versailles had been described as the eighth wonder of the world. Even today few people would deny that the words 'baroque palace' most often call to mind the palace of Versailles. Together with St Peters in Rome, Chartres Cathedral, the Taj Mahal, the Hagia Sophia, the Pyramids of Gizeh and a few other monuments, Versailles belongs to the undisputed masterpieces of world stature, the immortal heritage of mankind.

The aesthetic judgements of contemporaries, as well as of later historians of art and architecture, on the subject of Versailles are more conflicting than on any other great monument, and range from the greatest dislike, explicable only on ideological grounds, to unthinking raptures, and from Victor Hugo's crushing but at least socially perceptive description of the palace as 'barracks for courtiers', by way of the Duc de Saint-Simon's (1675–1755) bitter criticism, to the note written on a contemporary etching of Versailles by Perelle, which says, '*Le Château de Versailles . . . est admiré comme la plus belle et la plus magnifique maison du Monde*'.

Be that as it may, it can be objectively stated that Versailles—when compared to Vienna's Schönbrunn and Belvedere, for example—was the trend-setting model for palaces built during the era of European Absolutism. It was the focal centre of all the cultural, artistic and even political movements and ideas of the day. With the possible exception of the Jesuit Church in Rome, no other contemporary building wielded so much influence in Europe. Its size alone (the garden frontage, apart from anything else, is 600 yards long) puts it in a class by itself. And finally, its four creators, Le Nôtre (garden design) Le Vau and Mansart (architecture) and Le Brun (interior frescoes and paintings) made up a team whose gifted and fertile collaboration has never been equalled before or since, comparable only to the inspired harmony between the architect Palladio and the fresco-painter Veronese in their creation of the renaissance villas of Venice, or between Neumann and Tiepolo in the palace of Würzburg.

Even the most critical observer of Versailles must admit that its 250-year-old walls have seen not only the petty intrigues, scandals and rivalries that provide biographers with such amusing stories, but history itself, great events and moments when the world for a moment held its breath. Here in 1715 Louis XIV, the 'Sun of Europe' died, not without uttering solemn—and, no doubt, strictly authentic—last words to his people, his heir and his morganatic wife, Madame de Maintenon. In 1722, after the palace had been left unoccupied for seven years, his more amiable but less realistic successor, Louis XV, moved in, followed in 1774 by his phlegmatic grandson Louis XVI, little suited to kingship and married to pretty, capricious Marie Antoinette, daughter of the Empress Maria Theresa of Austria. In 1789 far, far too late, the poor, weak king summoned the States General to institute reforms in the vain hope of stemming the flood of revolution. It was in the same year that the rebellious Paris mob broke in and forced Louis to move to the capital, where later he and his queen were beheaded by the guillotine. In the Hall of Mirrors in 1871 Wilhelm I, King of Prussia, had himself proclaimed first Emperor of Germany. In 1919 the First World War was concluded there by the Treaty of Versailles, which most of the world saw as a long-overdue curbing of the

Prussian-officer State, but the Germans felt to be an 'infamous decree', the prelude of a fateful turn in German history that was to lead to total collapse in 1945.

Versailles: 'The sun of France', 'The dream of Nations' or 'A petrified symbol of royal despotism'?

Let us begin at the beginning. Louis XIV started the building of his new, his 'own' palace in 1661, the year in which the too puissant Cardinal Mazarin, his mother's lover, died. Psychological interpretations are not lacking. One could explain Versailles as the symbol of the son's triumph over his mother's lover. With Mazarin's death the last obstacle between Louis and absolute power had fallen. Now Versailles could be raised as an expression of that power and its pretensions. Of the young king's withdrawal from his capital and flight to the land, and their origin in the traumatic experiences of his youth, we have already spoken. For the future site of his dream palace he chose the swampy wasteland of Versailles, where Louis XIII had had a modest hunting lodge. Whether from filial piety or frugality—and the latter hardly seems likely—Louis XIV did not entirely demolish his father's house to build anew from the ground up, but mantled and surrounded it with technically and aesthetically new constructions. Because the original building by Solomon de Brosse (1624) had been preserved and, until 1670, only altered and extended by Le Vau, the proportions of the great forecourt with its 'diminishing perspective' were on a somewhat old-fashioned plan:

'The courtyard narrows in stages towards the back like a Gothic church porch, drawing the visitor progressively towards the principle entrance in the middle of the main frontage. Its resemblance to the front of a Greek temple gave the ritual of receiving guests a certain ceremonial solemnity. One is drawn into the entry like a fish into a fish-trap.'

(Richard Hamann)

In the middle of his long garden frontage on the other side Le Vau built a covered terrace above the ground floor between two blocks of building to vary yet unify the façade (carried out between 1668 and 1669). His design must have been far more spatially interesting, lively and handsome than the new version produced after 1680 by his successor Jules Hardouin-Mansart (1646–1708). Mansart enclosed Le Vau's terrace, the original 'apartement simple' to make the 70-metre-long Hall of Mirrors or *Grande Galerie* and marked its position on the outside of the façade with a row of six columns (1679–1684). Two big wings (plate 21) were also added to Le Vau's original building. Le Vau's design was not ruined, but in some respects it was decidedly watered down. A good many art historians grieve for the building's earlier appearance which was sacrificed for the sake of interior pomp and a great parade ground for courtiers, the *Grande Galerie* (pl. 24). So it is understandable if modern opinion, at the safe distance of two hundred years, avers that

'Costly though the palace is, greatly as it excels all comparable buildings in size and magnificence, it never achieves the charm and harmony of some other baroque palaces. ... Its walls may rise never so high, yet they always give the impression of a vast, expensive and decorative stage set.'

(Paul Barz, 1971)

This theatrical effect stems directly from the way in which the great pile grew up, like sediment formed by successive accretions of inner space and outer façade. It is like a gigantic onion made up of layer after layer: Louis XIII's hunting lodge the inner core, then Le Vau's building and finally

59 *Würzburg Palace: garden façade. The builder of this residence, the largest baroque palace in Germany outside Berlin, was Johann Philipp Franz, Count of Schönborn and Prince Bishop of Würzburg (1673–1724). The first plans, made in 1719, were the reslult of multiple consultations with the leading architects of Paris and Vienna, the centres of baroque building. The architect in charge, whose task was to unify the whole, was the Würzburger Director of Building, Balthasar Neumann, but he and his architecturally knowledgeable patron considered ideas from the Frenchmen, Robert de Cotte and Germain Boffrand, as well as from Prince Eugene's personal architect Lucas von Hildebrandt. The palace was built in three stages: 1719–1722, 1723–1729 and 1729–1746. Building, and especially the interior decoration, was not completed until the end of the 18th century. The heart and connecting point of the whole layout is the commanding central block housing the entrance hall and principal state rooms. The most striking feature of the long and otherwise rather flat garden façade is the projecting mass of this central pavilion, emphasized by the richness of its architectural embellishments: the paired columns, decorated window frames, crowning pediment and the flowing conformation of the roof.*

60 *Würzburg Palace: entrance hall. The ground-floor vestibule of the central block is so spacious that a coach-and-four could turn round in it. Free-standing double columns and grouped pillars form arches that support the flat ceiling. The hall leads to the foot of the main staircase. The coolly classical decoration is the work of the plasterer Ludovici Bossi, and was done between 1765 and 1766. Franz Anton Ärmeltraut painted the ceilings; the illusional, grisaille painting on the inside of the cupola depicts scenes from the life of Hercules. Only the atlantes on the pillars, the work of the Würzburger sculptor Johann Wofgang von Auwera (1749), give a whiff of rococo spirit to the otherwise sober classical atmosphere of the low-slung hall.*

Page 124:
61 *Würzburg Palace: adjacent to the entrance hall is the* sala terrana *or garden room designed by Balthasar Neumann in 1730. The bare walls were ready in 1741, at the same time as those of the Kaisersaal (Emperor's state room) above it, but the decoration was not completed until after 1749. Above an almost oval ground plan is a shallow dome. It is supported by an oval ring of slender marble columns near the wall, but leaving an open passage in between surmounted by its own series of arches and small domed ceilings, the whole conveying a feeling of lightness. At intervals along the sides are red marble pilasters in effective contrast to the white walls. Also white is the delicate stucco work by Antonio Bossi that curvingly overlaps the painted dome to where three-dimensional plaster* putti *seem to become part of the fresco. Johann Zick painted the richly toned ceiling in 1750. The mythological scenes depicted, 'Feast of the Gods' and 'Diana's Repose', have open-air settings to prepare us for the garden just outside.*

123

Mansart's definitive version with its endless garden wings out of all scale to human strides or bodies. They advance in military order and axial regularity as if in time to a drum beat, the columns forming fours and sixes, rising grandly from above the solid, rusticated ground floor, past the stately first storey and lesser mezzanine to the attic storey crowned with statuary (pl. 21, 22). There is something violent, heavy, oppressive about the architecture, a sense of immense effort, as if thrust and counterthrust, not yet quite held in leash, had been forced into the iron discipline of regimented squares. Everything one connects with baroque palace design—flowing lines, curving frontages, a dynamic composition of masses, all blithely heightened with exuberant ornament—seems to be undeveloped or suppressed, as if it contradicted the ideology of power the structure was created to express. Looking at the garden façades of Versailles, one sighs for the magic wand of a Neumann, Dientzenhofer, Lukas von Hildebrandt or Fischer von Erlach to bring the Sleeping Beauty to life.

Mansart's real achievement is the palace interior. As the designer of those central points of sunlight from which radiated the daily routine of the king and his court, namely the Chapel Royal (early morning) and the Hall of Mirrors (morning), his architectural innovations are epoch-making. It is hard to know which to admire more, his gifted touch as planner, designer and supervisor, or his talent for selecting the right men to assist him, above all Le Brun (1619–1690), the painter of murals and ceilings, who contributed no less to the 'miracle of Versailles' than Le Vau, Mansart and Le Nôtre.

The ceremonial function of the Hall of Mirrors, extending from the room depicting the destructive force of war at one end to that celebrating the creative power of peace at the other, has already been dealt with, as has also the special purpose of the looking-glass walls to extend the room into endless distances and multiply the bowing lines of courtiers *ad infinitum*; as well as the essential prerequisite of this theatrical setting: the establishment of a glass and mirror factory with Italian hands.

The *Grande Galerie* lies in the centre of the west-facing main garden front on the same axis as the true heart of the house, the king's bedchamber, facing east on to the forecourt (pl. 23, 25, 26). There, with the dawn appearing through the windows, the king got up for his ceremonial morning levée, symbol of the sunrise, the monarch being the sun who sent his beneficent rays into every corner of the great building.

The Chapel Royal of Versailles (pl. 27, 28) has justly been described as the most beautiful interior of the palace. Its construction was begun in 1688 on the order of Louis, who became more interested in religion as he grew older. It was not finished until 1703, because work was interrupted by the war resulting from the League of Augsburg. The old chapel had been in the central block. The new sacred building was in the north wing facing on to the forecourt, but was so planned that it could be reached directly from the king's first-floor apartments by a private passageway.

The soaring, two-tiered church with its rounded apse is reminiscent, in spite of all stylistic differences, of two buildings of the early and high Middle Ages respectively, that also served to glorify the State and the person of the monarch: the Palatine Chapel of Charlemagne in Aix-la-Chapelle and the Sainte-Chapelle of Saint Louis in Paris. In the latter case Mansart may well have been consciously influenced by a wish to bridge the 400-year gap between the two Louis.

The memory of the national Gothic style at the time of the king's saintly namesake and his most pious work (the Sainte-Chapelle) is mingled with that of the ancient Roman style it superseded. In this baroque version of the

Page 125:
62 *Würzburg Palace: the Kaisersaal (Emperor's Hall), the principal state room of the residence, is on the first floor, on the park side of the central block. The bare walls were ready in 1741 but, because money was short, the decoration could not be done till 1749–1753, in Prince Bishop Karl von Greiffenclau's time. He then commissioned the most prominent fresco painter of the age, the Venetian Giovanni Battista Tiepolo, who, with his paintings turned Balthasar Neumann's already handsome room into one of the most beautiful interiors in any European palace. Ranged at intervals along the walls are agate-coloured, three-quarter columns of marble, a material and colour especially beloved of baroque architects. The subtle tones of the columns are accentuated by their gilded bases and capitals. The soaring dome is pierced by deeply embrasured circular windows. It is less the architectural form, however, than the finely calculated colour scheme that creates such a breathtaking effect. While Tiepolo's magnificent frescoes, depicting events in the history of the bishopric, are the room's artistic triumph, the work of the stucco craftsman. Antonio Bossi, who fashioned the charming little figures in the wall-niches, should not be forgotten.*

63 *Würzburg Palace: the main staircase. Since the staircase was the centre of baroque ceremonial reception, it was logical for it to be placed in the heart of the building. This typically German feature reached its apogee in the great stairway at Würzburg. It becomes, indeed, the principal state room of the palace. From the low-slung entrance hall on the ground floor a single flight ascends to a halfway landing from which two parallel outer flights double back on the first one to reach an upper landing. From there the stairwell rises over the height of two storeys to an enormous cove-vaulted ceiling. It was an unusually large hall for its time, and few but Balthasar Neumann would have had the technical skill to create it. Today, unfortunately, it is not entirely as he designed it. Between 1765 and 1766, after his death, the stairs were decorated by Ludovico Bossi in a somewhat cold classical style that does not go too well with Tiepolo's ceiling.*

Sainte-Chapelle there is the same peripteros (clerestory) like a Corinthian temple built over a low arcade of Roman pillars.

The high arched, closely ranged windows below, together with the windows set in the vaulting above, produce a wonderful illumination. Light, indeed, becomes an intrinsic part of the structure, as in the best French Gothic. The wall colouring of white and gold and the gold running through the ceiling painting by Antoine Coypel contribute to the lighting effect. It is no wonder that this imposing, harmonious interior, where the king was regularly to be seen, composed and dignified but without pomp or false sentiment, had a pronounced effect on German baroque building, or that Balthazar Neumann, for instance, was deeply impressed by such a total work of art with its component parts of architecture, light, colour and painting.

The Gardens

The real 'miracle of Versailles', however, was not its exterior architecture—except perhaps the Chapel Royal—nor even its interior decoration, but the fairy-tale park designed by André le Nôtre (1613–1700). As a creator of Versailles, he has often been put before Le Vau, Mansart and le Brun. Louis XIV, having seen his first great work, the palace gardens of Vaux-le-Vicomte (1633–1660), commissioned him to design the park of Versailles. Apart from his artistic achievement, le Nôtre owed his royal summons, as did also Le Vau and Le Brun, to a personal circumstance. The young king was jealous of his over-powerful *Surintendant de Finances*, Nicolas Fouquet. When the latter built the Château de Vaux as an expression of political power, Louis felt his own position threatened. There the king acted as host at a summer party in 1660—on a borrowed stage, so to speak—and in 1661 he came to Vaux again to see the first performance of Molière's ballet '*Les Facheux*'. The king put a good face on it and concealed his fury at his chief treasury official being able to produce a display so brilliant as to outdo the royal court itself. Secretly, however, he was planning his minister's downfall. Soon after the Molière ballet Fouquet's hubris was punished. All his offices were taken from him; he was accused of fraud, corruption and embezzlement and thrown into prison. Colbert stepped into his shoes, and the king took over Fouquet's team of artists, Le Vau, Le Brun and Le Nôtre, to create Versailles for him. The glories of Vaux-le-Vicomte fell into oblivion.

Le Nôtre's task was a tremendous one both as to the size of the terrain and the artistic goal aimed at. An area of 3.5 by 2.5 kilometres, with axes up to seven kilometres long, was to be organized into a park that would form a unified aesthetic whole with the architectural scheme of the palace itself. Le Nôtre found a solution. The shapes and proportions into which he divided the land not only faithfully reflected the form and composition of the palace's vast mass of stone, but themselves assumed the character of an independent work of architecture. 'Without Le Nôtre's park,' says Hubala, 'the palace of Versailles would be a monstrosity.' With Le Nôtre garden design became a separate discipline within architecture, and the garden designer became a garden architect. Although the formal, geometrical park of the baroque era, generally known as the 'French style', was superseded in the 18th and 19th centuries by the romantic English landscape garden, with its apparently free and natural formation, the masterpiece that Le Nôtre created at Versailles in 1661 soon became a model for every park in Europe.

Le Nôtre's aim was to 'put Nature to shame by means of Art'. Huge masses of soil were moved, water was brought from a distance, canals were cut, great

Pages 128–129:
64 *Würzburg Palace: the White Drawing Room or* Salle d'Armes. *Between the main staircase and the Kaisersaal comes the White Drawing Room, intended perhaps as a restful transition zone between the colourful frescoes and architectural splendours of the stair case and the equally magnificent Kaisersaal. The whole room is coloured in white and off-white, broken only by the subtle contrasts of the brown doors and grey-black stove. The glory of the room is the exquisite, lacy stucco work on walls and ceiling, wrought by Antonio Bossi in only a few months during 1744. It is rococo decoration at its best.*

65 *Würzburg Palace: A view of the east part of the gardens. A section of the old town fortifications blocks the view. To make the best of the space available a circular scheme was chosen. A central lawn with paths is surrounded by a box hedge in the form of an arcaded walk opening out on to a view of terraces and ramparts.*

66   Munich, Nymphenburg Palace: the park front. In 1664 Adelaide of Savoy, wife of the Prince Elector Ferdinand Maria of Bavaria, decided to have a pleasure palace with park built near Munich, the town of their royal residence. An Italian, Agostino Barelli, was chosen as architect. To suit the allegorical-mythological fashion of the time, the name of the place was changed from Hofmark Kemnath to Castello delle Ninfe (Castle of the Nymphs), which rendered into German is Nymphenburg. The Bolognese Barelli (1627–1687), known for his designs for the Munich Theatiner Church, planned the building as a cubic pavilion, its original relationship to Italian villa architecture is now almost unrecognisable. After 1671 the comparatively modest palace was surrounded by a small garden with star-shaped lawns. In 1674 Enrico Zucalli (1652–1724) became Director of Building and exercised a considerable influence on the final form of the palace. At the behest of Prince Elector Maximilian II he and Giovanni Antonio Viscardi together extended the central pavilion with four further connected pavilions, two on each side. In 1715 their Paris-trained successor, Josef Effner (1687–1745), added a French touch to the hitherto purely Italian creation. It was the Elector himself, however, who was responsible for the total effect, in that he insisted on Barelli's great central block remaining the dominating feature of the whole composition.

132

basins dug out, miles of avenues and intersecting paths laid down, thousands of trees, hedges and shrubs transplanted. It is estimated that at the height of the building activity in Versailles Palace and garden up to 30,000 people were employed at any one time, and that the total turnover of workers during those years was over 100,000. It is no invention that, during the building of an enormous canal that was never completed, thousands of workers died from epidemics and the bad climate. The triumphant completion of the whole great undertaking seemed justification enough and the sacrifices were forgotten.

Le Nôtre's raw material was nature and her elements: masses of earth flattened or piled up into terraces, flowing, gushing water for canals and fountains, calm, mirrored water for large ponds or artificial basins, greenery transported and propped-up, brightly coloured flowers changing season by season, natural stone in many shades for edging, garden walls, groups of statuary, and all sorts of sand and gravel for laying paths and making decorative inlays. From these basic materials he fashioned the ideal palace grounds in the French style, with their canonical sequence of lawns, flower-beds and water near by the palace, the shrubbery to the west and finally the park and hunting area. The whole layout was determined by the long stretches of canal and avenue radiating outwards into the far distance. One can see that this star-like ground plan influenced a whole generation of baroque planners, whether one thinks of Karlsruhe (after 1715), Rastatt, the road system of the Place d'Etoile (called Place de Gaulle since 1970) in Paris or Enfant's design for the new capital at Washington (1791).

The whole vast composition, an architectural manipulation of nature into an incomparable stage set, draws foreground and distance into masterly unison, making the palace the centre of the world, and the king's bedroom, its innermost cell, the meeting point of the star's ten rays (seven axes on the park side, three great avenues radiating out towards the town) the very heart of the solar system.

To relieve the monotony of the flat landscape, Le Nôtre made skilful use of the mound of earth dug from the palace foundations, using it as a basis for the terrace and steps leading to the gardens (pl. 31). In front of the grand western façade on the park side he excavated a semi-circular arena, the former *Fer à Cheval*, in the south he placed the orangery and to the north a huge stepped cascade reminiscent of 16th century Italian gardens such as those of the Villa d'Este in Tivoli and at Caprarola Palace, where such ornamental waters were suggested by the natural lay of the land.

From the commanding height of the terrace one sees the arrangement of the park as a system of viewpoints and vistas all delightful, whether one looks back towards the palace or outwards into the distance, or at charming details in the foreground, such as pools, fountains and hedge-screened theatres or the highly artificial embroidery of flowerbeds, topiary and trelliswork.

Works of Art

Not only was Le Nôtre's park distinguished by the most varied formal and aesthetic qualities, all related to the architecture of the palace; it also contained works of art which were esoteric references to the kingdom, the State and the sovereign himself. The *Bassin d'Encelade* contrived by Gaspard Marsy in 1675 is adorned by a lead statue of Eskalados, the giant defeated by Hercules. Hercules was a favourite figure in the baroque allegory of princes, the Greek hero standing for the founder of his State, a role to which Louis XIV, as progenitor of the 'new' absolutist France, was by no means averse.

67 *Munich, Nymphenburg Palace: park front of the central pavilion (1664–1675). Princess Adelaide's pleasure palace has not come down to us exactly as it was first built. In 1715 her son, Maximilian II, Elecotor of Bavaria, had it altered inside and out. The original balanced, if slightly boring rows of windows seen in old pictures of the building were broken up by a redecoration of the entrance façade. Four Corinthian pilasters now ran up from first floor to attic storey, enriching the composition and pulling it together. The façade was further differentiated from the two side sections by the addition on the first and second floors of two rows of three big-arched windows, which also provide more light for the central state room, several storeys high.*

134

68 *Munich, Nymphenburg Palace: bedroom in the south wing. The oldest part of the decoration is the 1675 painting on the central oval of the baroque ceiling. Most of the remaining furnishings, such as the 1720 chimneypiece in French* régence *style, belong to the 18th century. Other objects are from the later Rococo period in the second half of the century. A richly inlaid writing desk was made in 1760; the two commodes date from about 1775. The green velvet bed canopy embroidered in gold thread belongs to the early 18th century. Copied from old patterns, the damask wall-lining was made and hung in 1963.*

137

He also appears in other parts of Versailles, such as the central decoration of the forecourt façade, where, in partnership with Mars, he supports a clock in the form of the sun. Mars too was a personification of Louis XIV, whose glorious deeds of war had united his country and brought it new renown. Thus the whole design symbolizes the conquest of time (the clock), space and the world.

The figures decorating the big *Bassin des Eaux de France* represent the chief rivers of the land and show the extent of France and of Louis' territorial greatness. On another important fountain there is a statue of Neptune, probably symbolizing the king's claim to supremacy not only in the North Atlantic adjacent to France's coast, and the western Mediterranean, but also in colonial waters. Still half immersed in the waters of the most magnificent basin in Versailles rises the chariot of Apollo harnessed to four plunging horses. Situated directly to the east of the king's bedroom, it is an allegorical reference to the sunrise and to the levée of the 'new Apollo'.

A typical example of baroque iconology is provided by the *Grand Escalier* also known as the Ambassador's Staircase, built between 1672 and 1680, removed by Louis XV, but now restored to its original form with the help of old plans and engravings. Right in the centre, dominating the stair well, is a bust of Louis XIV below a head of Apollo, divinity of the Muses, god of music, learning and husbandry. Now Louis has been promoted to Apollo Musagetes and is seen as the patron of the Muses, who, like water, perpetually renews himself and makes the whole world fertile. Accordingly, a fountain gushes out below the statue, while Louis' divine command of the four quarters of the globe is illustrated by four large murals depicting the American Indians, the Europeans, the Africans and the Asiatics. But nothing is gained without effort: conquest and dominion come by the sword. Thus four huge tapestries designed by Le Brun show Louis as warlord (Cambrai, Valenciennes, St Omer and Cassel, 1677). On the painted ceiling, on the other hand, we see the king as Prince of Peace, patron of learning and the arts.

In connection, perhaps, with his claim to world encircling omnipotence, the Sun King had an astralobe set up on the terrace running along the west front. Later—after 1680—it was removed to make way for the big ornamental pond, but an even larger replacement was erected in his château of Marly, where he often stayed.

The ornamental waters, second theme of Le Nôtre's garden design, might almost be, with their mirror-like surfaces, the horizontal projection or counterpart of the *Grande Galerie*. Once again the smooth, shining reflections of the light make a happy metaphor for the Sun King's radiance.

If one is familiar with the natural philosophy and view of the universe that the baroque age inherited from the Renaissance, it seems reasonable to suppose—as suggested in the theory of Franzsepp Würtenberger—that a palace and park such as Versailles were thought of as a world in miniature and centre of the universe, just as the Italians of an earlier generation explicitly regarded their palaces and villas. The palace precincts constituted a functioning organism complete in itself. The area of palace grounds of the Versailles type was no more than eight to ten square kilometres, but within that space the baroque designer sought to represent by symbol and sample the Earth in its entirety. The natural, chaotic, outside world was condensed to a sphere of controlled elegance and order.

Olympia was present everywhere in Versailles, inside as well as out. The lower regions of Greek mythology, the underworld ruled by Orpheus, was represented in the park by artificial caverns and grottos, and in the palace by the *sala terrena*, the cool, ground floor garden room, giving directly on to the gardens. Next we come to the realm of the lower creation, the plants and animals. Flower-beds, tree-lined avenues, lawns, outdoor theatre, green-houses for rare plants, as well as sculptured decorations of vases, garlands, flowers and festoons of fruit, all in stone, with their attendant cherubs, belong to the first group. The second is represented by living creatures in zoo and aviary, hounds in the dog-run, horses in the stables, carvings of animals in the park and paintings of them indoors. Next above them in rank are the major and minor divinities, either as garden sculptures or depicted on walls and ceilings: Flora, Pomona, Vertumnus, Diana, Hercules, Mercury, Jupiter and Juno, Apollo and Minerva. Purely symbolic features such as the maze described above, or a pavilion-crowned 'hill of virtue', an allegory of man's hard ascent to salvation, complete the picture.

There were still other allegorical figures in the garden world, among them the four winds, the four elements and the already mentioned *Bassin des Eaux de France* with its French rivers to underline the extent of the king's dominion. All these attractions were inter-connected by a network of well-tended avenues and paths. What the leading architectural theoretician of early baroque Italy, Vincenzo Scamozzi, said in 1615 applies equally well to Versailles.

'The axial avenues that lead up to villas and country seats must be wider and more beautiful than others, for they are a sign of high rank. They must afford delightful views from higher ground and run very straight so that the mansion can be seen without hindrance from afar. Also, for reasons of lordliness, they should be broad and on a grand scale'.

The Grand Trianon

Louis XIV moved to the countryside to escape from the gloomy Louvre, official business and the townsfolk, whom he looked on only as a rabble; but it was not long before public life caught up with him. The ritual routine and the perpetual bustle at court became a burden. The king's life, at his levée, at dinner or elsewhere, was spent entirely in public under the eyes of multitudes of onlookers. Even when the queen had a baby all the doors of the birth-chamber had to be open. So, barely six or seven years after the final move to Versailles on the 6th of May, 1682, the king conceived the idea of building a private, intimate, little summer palace where he could take refuge from time to time. It was called Trianon after the hamlet that had once stood there but was now demolished. And the Grand Trianon, built as a quiet retreat from Versailles, was thought by some connoisseurs to be far superior to the big palace (pl. 33, 34, 35).

Hardouin-Mansart obtained this commission too. As with the main palace, there was already a building on the site, which is worth a short description for its unique charm, although we only know it from engravings and reports. In 1670 Le Vau had erected what for those days passed for quite a modest pavilion. It was intended for intimate little parties at the end of a long walk in the park. To keep up with the craze for the exotic, the walls had been lined from floor to ceiling with the prettiest pottery tiles hand-painted in bright colours in fashionable Chinese, Turkish and Persian patterns. The tiles were made in the king's own pottery at St Cloud from a secret recipe. At that time the mystery of 'white gold' was known only in the East, and oriental potters were careful not to divulge it. Another use for the pavilion was as a storage place for the swiftly accumulating collection of gifts, mostly porcelain and pottery, brought by ambassadors from the Near and Far East. Madame de Montespan, the *maitresse en titre* of the day, was delighted with the exotic,

139

70 *Munich, Nymphenburg Palace: A bedroom in the south wing. This apartment too was decorated in 1810. Typical of the period is the combination of mahogany with gilded bronze, plated or inlaid and used to enhance the chaste elegance of the furniture. The gold swan's necks supporting the chair-arms anticipate the* Art Nouveau *of a century later. The room has a special interest in that Ludwig II, King of Bavaria, was born there on the 25th of August, 1845.*

magical summerhouse that had been dedicated to her. It was reminiscent of the tiled and encrusted courts of Arabia. The renown of the porcelain palace soon spread abroad and it was copied all over Europe.

Louis' love for La Montespan was transient and grew cold. When he saw that the fragile materials of Trianon were beginning to deteriorate too after only ten years he took it as an omen. The delicate tiles cracked and split in the cold of winter. So in 1687 the porcelain house was knocked down and the new marble Trianon began to rise in its place, dedicated to the new *maitresse en titre*, Madame de Maintenon. The Marble Trianon possessed all the charm and grace that was somehow lacking from Versailles. Mansart had added a new element to his architecture: colour. The outside walls are of warm, yellowish limestone from Troissy, vertically divided at regular intervals by pilasters in lovely white-veined pink marble that came from Languedoc. The columns of the arcaded front are greenish white Carrara marble, but the marble capitals and bases are snow-white. Altogether it is a ravishing colour scheme (pl. 34, 35). It says something of the good taste and dignified bearing of Liselotte van der Pfalz, the sister-in-law and long the bosom friend of the king, that after his death she took up permanent residence at Trianon and loved it above anywhere else. She died there in 1722.

At Trianon Louis could lead a private life and indulge in the passion for botany that he shared with so many other baroque noblemen. There he was a 'landed gentleman' who took an interest in his *potager royal*, the fruit and vegetable garden that was planted near the house. Above all, it was the scene of his moving friendship with his garden designer, Le Nôtre, and his chief botanist, La Quintinie. Through their common botanical studies Le Nôtre, so talented yet never haughty, and La Quintinie, a simple but distinguished soul, both such contrasts to the sycophants at court, had grown dear to the king's heart. They would all three stroll together, dressed in plain country clothes, through Le Nôtre's plantations and La Quintinie's greenhouses, discussing their latest exotic imports. Japanese sophoras, cedars of Lebanon, magnolias, rhododendrons, azaleas, the Mexican begonia and Chinese chrysanthemum were acclimatized and domesticated. A special greenhouse was built for the king's favourite delicacy, the fig. The three friends did botanical research together. In one year no fewer than 18 million tulip bulbs were imported from Holland for planting and experiment. Flower arrangements were changed each season, or sometimes, to please the royal family, several times a day by growing blooms in special stone tubs. In 1694 Le Nôtre reported that there were two million flowering plants at Trianon, that no dead leaf was ever seen and that there was always something in bloom there, even in the winter months. Until Louis' death it was counted a high honour to be invited to join the little circle in Trianon.

Louis XV meant the Grand Trianon to be a retreat for the love of his old age, the beautiful and intelligent Madame d'Etoiles, otherwise known as the Marquise de Pompadour. After a failed attempt on his life was made there in 1757, however, he took a dislike to the place and had another miniature palace built in quite a different style in another part of the grounds. It became known as the Petit Trianon. The marble Trianon lay deserted until its furnishings were destroyed during the revolution. Napoleon renovated the palace and presented it to his mother, but she never felt comfortable there, perhaps because the splendid decorations of the Empire period did not suit it. Then, in 1837, Louis Phillippe, the 'bourgeois king', moved in, ripped down walls and filled it with vulgar, ostentatious furniture in the taste of the day. Finally, General de Gaulle had the Grand Trianon splendidly restored and redecorated to serve as a government guest-house for distinguished visitors.

Petit Trianon and Le Hameau

In the Grand Trianon Louis XIV found refuge from Versailles. The Petit Trianon was Louis XV's retreat—from the overwhelming shadow of his great predecessor, whose presence was all too evident even in the larger summer residence. Times and tastes had changed.

'This man of narrow elegance shuddered when he thought of the long, broad avenues of Versailles, where one felt small and lost.'

(M. L. Gothein)

In the eyes of Louis XV Le Nôtre's garden plans seemed on the large side, even at the Marble Trianon.

So Louis gave way to La Pompadour's pleas for a *buon ritiro* of her own arranged according to her taste. Every appearance of pomp and monumentality was to be avoided. Naturalness, utility, populism were the catchwords of the day, the declining years of Rococo. The last not in the modern political sense, of course, but meaning a populace of dainty shepherdesses and Arcadian shepherds. *'Une menagérie d'utilité plus que de curiosité'* was Pompadour's wish, so instead of unusual and exotic creatures, there were useful domestic ones: a well-stocked poultry yard, a herd of Dutch cows, and consequently a dairy.

Le Nôtre's successor, Gabriel, created a pleasant garden, but on a smaller, more intimate scale to suit the fashionable taste. Louis XV himself helped to draw up the plans, just as his contemporary, Frederick the Great, did at Sanssouci. Le Nôtre's garden was completely screened off by means of great rows of trees. In 1749 a garden pavilion had been started and by 1751 it was ready. The Petit Trianon Palace itself was built 1671–73. The royal treasury accounts are so detailed that we know precisely what the building cost: 736,056 livres, 16 sols, 6 deniers. The chapel was completed in 1772, shortly before the king's death.

In Louis XVI's reign court life became concentrated in the Petit Trianon. When he came to the throne he presented the little palace to his queen, Marie Antoinette, with a pretty speech in the affectedly simple style of the time, 'Since you love flowers, I have a little bouquet I should like to give you. Take the Petit Trianon'. In matters of taste it was the court that was up to date and set the trend. What trend was so in fashion then, and whose words did they learn by heart?

The answer is Jean-Jacques Rousseau (1712–1778), the rationalist whose social criticism and ideas ultimately superseded the Bourbon age of Enlightenment and banished the ghost of the great Sun King. His basic thesis was that man is naturally good; he remains good only so long as he remains natural; he becomes bad when he does not obey his feelings. The degeneration of culture and civilization (thus envy, lies and dissembling) is the result of two much reflection. Rousseau's slogan, found in his *Emile* (1762) and especially in his novel *La Nouvelle Heloise* (1761), was 'Back to Nature' back to the simple 'education of the heart' and of feeling as opposed to reason. So, as the baroque age gave way to the New Era, people felt that life and its surroundings should be simpler and more natural—and the royal family was no exception. One should stroll through gardens along winding lanes and paths, not down sternly regal avenues, but as in a picture gallery, wandering from one lovely landscape to another: from stately trees, solitary or growing in natural-seeming groups to romantic outcrops of rock, mossy caves half hidden in the dusky woods, little temples, memorial stones, ruins, unexpected springs or rippling streams running into some silent lily pond edged with banks of grass, not stone. A park should be a place where, in a

Pages 146–147:
71 *Munich, Nymphenburg Palace: King Ludwig I's Gallery of Beauties in the south wing. It was originally Queen Caroline's dining room, but was later filled with 38 female portraits painted by J. Stieler between 1827 and 1850 on the orders of the king. The famous beauties immortalized by Stieler were not, as they would have been in the baroque age, all nobly born ladies of the court, but were drawn from all ranks of society, showing that ideas of beauty were growing more democratic. At least one of the women portrayed – the supposedly Spanish dancer, Lola Montez – has a place in history, for it was her liaison with Ludwig I that sparked off the riots of 1848 which finally cost the king his throne.*

sunny clearing among the trees, a lover and his lass might chance upon the home of a humble cottager who would offer them a bowl of milk fresh from the cow and prepare tham a couch of twigs and rose-petals among the grass. Reality was submerged in romance, in 'feeling'. Today, we might call it nostalgia for a world that never was.

It was no longer the baroque garden architect who set the tone, but the landscape painter. Trees, rocks, ponds, sloping lawns and serpentine paths were grouped from a purely picturesque point of view. The new fashion came from England which, for political and social reasons, had more or less 'skipped' the exuberant geometry of the absolutist High Baroque to land in the late eighteenth century as artistic leader, especially in the design of gardens. On his new garden plan of 1774 Marie Antoinette's personal gardener Antoine Richard wrote '*Project pour le jardin Anglo-Chinois du Petit Trianon*'. And although that poetic publicist for the English garden in France, the Abbé de Lilles, with his French feeling for tradition and continuity regretted the demise of the baroque gardens in Versailles, 'that masterpiece wrought by a great king, Le Nôtre and the age', he found the absolutist world monotonous. The geometrical garden seemed to him 'no subject for a poem'. 'The old gardens', he maintained, 'were those of architects; the new are those of philosophers, painters and poets'. A leading painter of the time, Hubert Robert, called on to design a feature for the 'little' Trianon, produced fourteen different sketches for a romantic, contrived arrangement of rocks with a waterfall and belvedere pavilion in the woods.

The first project made for the 'new' Petit Trianon was the small *Théatre de la Reine*, where Glück's 'Iphigenia on Tauris' had its first performance. In 1778 a rather sentimental structure, the *Temple d'Amour* , a rotonda with marble Corinthian columns, was built on an artificial island in the middle of a pond in the park (pl. 38). Lastly came *Le Hameau* (p. 36, 37), a little 'model village' (1783–1786) where the queen and her ladies could play at being peasants, shepherdesses, gardeners or dairymaids. The 'Queen's House' (pl. 36) had a small dining-room and a games room for playing trictrac (a board game) and a Chinese closet. It was joined by an olive-green panelled passage to a billiard room. There were also an artificial watermill, a dairy, cowstalls and servants' quarters. The domestic staff, kept to a minimum, had its own little house. A 'real' peasant with his wife, a groom and a maid were specially engaged—we even know his name: Valy Bussard. A Swiss soldier, Jean Bersy, was the only bodyguard. A gardener by the name of Bréval saw to the flowers and fruit trees. The queen had insisted on *useful* fruits such as nuts, plums, apricots and peaches; by her wish a kitchen garden was added in 1784. To give the hamlet a truly natural look, two illusional painters were hired to add artificial signs of age and weathering to the buildings: falling plaster, patches of rustic brickwork, damp stains and even moss.

The anglicization of the Trianon gardens was not only a consequence of aesthetic change, but also a side-effect of political diplomacy. Relations between England and France, which had grown very cool during the American War of Independence (France had supported the rebels), gradually improved. Ambassadors were exchanged in 1783, and on July 22nd 1783 the British envoy, the Duke of Manchester, was invited to an evening reception in the anglicized gardens of the Petit Trianon. The ambassador must have felt very much at home there, and glad to see that France had at least an artistic leaning towards his country. As a chivalrous gesture of good will the Duke procured for the queen a treasure worth its weight in gold—an English gardener. His name was John Eggleton and he received a yearly salary of 300 guineas, a sum then comparable to the pay of a Real Madrid footballer today. A few weeks later the treaty that heralded the birth of the United States of America was signed in Versailles on September 3rd 1783.

The last little dinner parties given by the royal family took place in Le Hameau in 1789, the year of the great revolution. Then the whole garden dream life came to an end. As the Abbé de Lilles put it, 'It was like a work by Poussin. He painted a merry shepherds' dance, and by the dancers a grave inscribed "I too once lived in Arcady"'. Did the queen on her last sad journey to the scaffold think for a moment of her Arcadian fairyland in the Trianon grounds? We shall never know.

'No menacing voices from the approaching revolution penetrated to the gently rippling lake beside whose bank they played at blindman's buff, or to the pretty rotonda on its shore from where the god of love looked down on their nimble figures. The splendid clumps of trees around the lake grew tall and still. . . . Nearby, Versailles slept the sleep of giants, slept through all the dangers that threatened it, until it was safe to rise again; and now the idyll of the little Trianon seems simply one more jewel in its regalia.' (M. L. Gothein)

Schönbrunn Palace, Vienna

The first set of plans for Schönbrunn Palace was never used. It was the second series, prepared by the Architect Royal, Bernhard Fischer von Erlach, between 1693 and 1694, that was actually carried out on the orders of Emperor Leopold I, who intended the palace for his son, Joseph I, King of Rome. Building began in 1696 and came to a temporary halt when the central block was completed in the year 1700. In 1713 the two wings, part of which had been inhabited by the late emperor's widow since 1712, were finished except for the roof. The incomplete building passed into the possession of Charles VI in 1728 for the sum of 450,000 guilders. The new emperor pursued the project so energetically that by 1732 the palace was ready. Only a few years later, in 1739, new work on Schönbrunn was put in hand, including alterations to the roof area. The plan for a loggia surmounted by an equestrian statue was dropped in favour of a low attic storey. In 1744–1749, however, a new architect, Nikolaus Pacassi, organized some radical alterations both inside and out which considerably changed Fischer von Erlach's original conception. Instead of the flat roof first projected, the present sloping roof was built; balconies were added and the central domed room was done away with.

Todays observer may well be struck by the disproportion of the frontage. The wide wings overpower the middle section so that, in spite of its projecting attic structure, it looks inadequate, and the whole building appears to lack a dominating central point (pl. 49). The fault can be traced back to the first change of plan, when, on the 'advice' of Leopold I, the originally modest construction was enlarged by the addition of two wings arranged round square courtyards. In today's palace the boundary line between the building first planned and the extension ordered from on high is plain to see.

If, in the mind's eye, we cut away the outer wings from the central part, we get a good impression of Fischer's well-balanced original design which, in proportion, compactness and artistic quality far excels the final version. On the forecourt side (pl. 50) the stepped façade gives rise to seventeen different axes, the five central ones marked by arcade openings on the ground floor and carried upwards by a six-pillared colonnade. The vertical line of the middle section is continued into the projecting attic storey and finished off with a balustrade. (Fischer's first plan for the top floor had been a composition of columns and arches surmounted by an equestrian statue of Leopold I, something in the nature of the extravagant triumphal arches of which he was so fond.) The projecting side blocks are subordinated to the central part by having an even number of axes and no distinguishing arcades, columns, roof superstructures or external stairs.

The harmony of Fischer's design is disturbed, however, by the still further projecting outer wings added later, which, possessing an uneven number of axes, have a central section, marked by a colonnaded portico, that stands out against the flattened pilasters of the inner wings and even rivals the emphasis of the building's real centre.

The garden façade (pl. 49) is differently arranged. The line of the ground plan is much straighter than at the front, which almost resembles a *cour d'honneur*. The wall relief, too, is flatter. The façade's three-dimensional volume is still further reduced by the complete absence of colonnades. The central section is emphasized vertically by seven tall, arched french windows. As in the forecourt frontage, the extended wings rather overwhelm the middle section, but at least their central axes are marked only by flattened paired pilasters.

Inside the palace, in place of the cupola room demolished in the 1744–1749 alterations, a long, rectangular hall was built in the middle of the main block, stretching all the way through from forecourt to garden front. On the forecourt side the hall leads into long suites of rooms on each side extending right across the courtyard, whereas the suites running along the garden side are quite short.

At its far end, the forecourt is bordered with stabling, low, simply constructed buildings attached to the entrance lodges and harmonised with them by means of double pilasters like those on the ground floor of the palace. Being purely utility constructions, they are completely subordinated to the whole.

The curved outside stairway (pl. 50) on the forecourt front serves not only for access to the first floor, but also to emphasize the importance of the central axis and make the main block look wider. It is repeated on the garden front, but on a smaller scale, in accordance with its lesser importance. This leads into the great central hall.

The gardens (pl. 49, 51, 52) are laid out in the French manner, with a pronounced central axis. The long stretch of lawn and avenue leading from the mansion comes to an abrupt halt where the Neptune Fountain (pl. 53) blocks its way. Beyond that a wide slope of lawn bordered with trees directs the gaze upward to the skyline on which stands a building of colonnades open to light and air, the so-called 'Gloriette' (pl. 51). It is at once a viewing point or, from the palace, the end of a vista.

The Upper and Lower Belvedere

In 1683 the young Prince Eugene of Savoy finally drove the Turks back from the gates of Vienna and with that victory rose like a comet to become Commander-in-Chief of the western forces. Ten years later, in 1693, the prince acquired some land to build a palace in the imperial capital, but outside the ring of fortifications, in the position from whence the besieging Turkish army had formerly aimed their cannon at the city. It took seven years of terracing work to render the sloping site fit for building. Then in 1702 a dividing wall was built to split it into an upper and a lower half. Between 1714 and 1716 a summer palace in the style of a garden belvedere was designed by Lukas von Hildebrandt, Chief Master Builder to the prince, and began to take shape in the lower part of the elongated site. Owing to inadequate source material the story of the planning of the Upper Belvedere is largely unknown. Only the start of building operations in 1721 and the completion of the bare brickwork in 1722 are reliably documented. Collaborating with Lukas von Hildebrant were Claudius le Fort du Plessy, interior decorator, and Le Nôtre's pupil, Girard, the garden architect and designer of ornamental waters.

The appearance of the Belvedere palaces and gardens was meticulously recorded in Solomon Kleiner's collection of copperplates published in 1731 and entitled 'The Astounding Seat of Battle and Victory ... or the exact Plans and Description of the Court, Pleasure Palace and Gardens ... Eugenii Francisci. ...' This typically baroque reproduction of a prodigious building project was dedicated to the glory of the architect's patron and not, as one would expect today, to that of the architect himself. However, the copper engravings are valuable evidence for anyone trying to reconstruct the original layout.

The Lower Belvedere, a 'mixture of suburban villa and orangery' (H.

73 Munich, Nymphenburg Palace: Amalienburg. In 1734–1739 the court architect, François Cuvilliès (1695–1768) designed a hunting lodge for the Princess Amalia, wife of the Bavarian Elector, in the spacious, French-style grounds of Nymphenburg. Cuvilliès was considered the 'wittiest and most graceful decorator of German Rococo' (Braunfels). The Wittels-bach monarch, Maximilian II, had discovered Cuvilliès' talent while in exile in the Netherlands. In 1708 the Elector brought the gifted Cuvilliès back to his own land, where he was honoured as the unsurpassed court decorator of splendour-loving Bavaria. Next to Munich's Cuvilliès Theatre (named after him) the best testimony to his playfully charming talent is the little Amalienburg pavilion. A single-storey building of modest proportions, it has an unusual ground-plan. The central reception room, which has a shallow dome rising slightly above the rest of the building, curves gently forward from the front façade. At the back there is a corresponding curve inwards, forming a miniature cour d'honneur. This arrangement gives the façade a lively line all the more noticeable

for the economy of its ornament. Over the main door is a figure of Diana the huntress; busts of satyrs have been placed in the rondels between the windows. The crowning glory of this elegant but restrained hunting lodge is the ravishing interior, a masterpiece in which stucco-worker, wood-carver and painter worked as one.

Keller), has remained outwardly untouched. It was intended as a summer residence for the prince, a bachelor who spent most of his life on the battlefields of Europe. The place was seldom inhabited. Inside, the sequence of reception rooms is continually interrupted by orangeries, giving the park front its wide, stretched-out appearance. So great is the width that it practically shuts off the gardens as if it were a wall. From a distance the attractive shape of the central pavilion's roof gives the Lower Belvedere great charm. Directly opposite this first palace, at the other end of the same long axis, stands the Upper Belvedere.

The Upper Belvedere, begun half a decade after the first palace, stands at the higher end of the elongated rectangle of formal garden that ascends to it by way of a series of terraces. Hildebrandt was in the happy position of having plenty of money to spend on his project and never having to modify his artistic ideas for the want of it. Practical requirements were not very demanding either, for when Prince Eugene was there at all he resided in the lower palace. For the realization of artistic aims that was a favourable circumstance.

Except for the central section, both forecourt and garden fronts are the same overall shape (pl. 43). The flatness of the long façades is broken up by the polygonal blocks in the middle and at both ends. In elevation the frontage is varied less by the difference in the façades than by the flowing curves of the roof profile. The three middle blocks are a storey higher than the domed octagons at the end of the wings, but continuity of line is ensured by the roof contours and the horizontal lines of the cornices. An arched porch, larger windows and greater height differentiate the central pavilion from the others.

On the forecourt side is a central entrance porch with three rounded arches. Two ramps, one on each side, lead into the slightly raised entrance hall (pl. 48) from which two short flights of stairs ascend to the landing outside the principal state apartment, the Marble Hall. Between these two parallel flights a central stairway goes down to the *sala terrena* or garden room (pl. 46), which leads into the open air. The considerable distance separating the upper and lower palaces is underlined by their facing one another on the same axis. Such a scheme was never repeated in any later baroque building plan. It was, however, a part of Hildebrandt's professional dogma. He and his great rival, Balthasar Neumann, both began as festival designers. That predisposed him to arrange architectural compositions in great open spaces, to harmonise buildings, and in his later work to plan in terms of extensive, processional axes and deeply recessed architectural units, ordered and bordered by set pieces of garden design such as ramps, walls and outdoor staircases. Nowhere is open space so convincingly integrated with architecture as in the Upper Belvedere. The principle goes back to the Genoese palaces where, in the same way, the stair well and the garden room were transition zones between interior and outside world. The relatively low, white-stuccoed rooms are in sharp contrast to the multi-coloured splendour of the high-ceilinged Marble Hall, the excessive ornament and costly materials of which are intended to express princely status.

A squarish forecourt (pl. 43) is a thematic introduction to the gardens lying between the Upper and Lower Belvederes. French models (the châteaux of Vaux-le-Vicomte and Versailles) were followed in Vienna under the direction of Dominique Girard, a pupil of Le Nôtre. The difference in altitude between the two palaces was skilfully used to heighten the impact of the Upper Belvedere. Two separate terraces served to divide the grounds of the two palaces and yet to emphasize their essential unity. Thus the high-lying palace is visible from every part of the grounds; the main axis, bordered with trees,

153

74 *Munich, Nymphenburg Palace:
Amalienburg, a glimpse of the Mirror Room.
In contrast to the almost plain exterior of the
hunting lodge, the inside is all glittering
splendour. In this room German Rococo
decoration reached a peak of imaginative
richness, variation and formal grace.*

75

75 *Pommersfelden, Weissenstein Palace:
entrance façade. It was the original intention
of Count Lothar Franz von Schönborn, Prince
Bishop of Bamberg and Elector of Mainz, that
his palace begun at Pommersfelden near
Bamberg in 1711 should be for his private use.
The busy diplomat and prince of the church
wanted a place far from political and ecclesiastical concerns, where he could pursue his
many personal interests as a private man.
Being one of the greatest art patrons of his
day, he included in his new palace a gallery for*
*contemporary paintings, to which he later
added an equally remarkable collection of
oriental porcelain. Today, with its unaltered
series of richly decorated state rooms, the
interior of Pommersfelden is an impressive
display of palatial culture in the baroque age.
As well as Johann Dientzenhöfer, who made
the original plans in 1711 and supervised the
building operations, Maximilian von Welsch,
and Lukas von Hildebrandt, architect to
Prince Eugene, contributed a good deal to the
undertaking with plans and advice.*

76 *Pommersfelden, Weissenstein Palace:
The undisputed high point of the whole palace
is the main stair-well, largely designed by von
Hildebrandt from an idea of his Schönborn
patron, and carried out by Dientzenhofer in
1718. The unusually spacious stair well is
surrounded by two galleries. Leading to the
first-floor landing and gallery is a double
staircase ascending with several turns from the
ground floor. From the balustrades of the
lower gallery fluted Corinthian columns rise to
the floor above. The upper gallery on this
second floor is a sort of arcade decorated with
atlantean figures.*

guides the eye directly towards it. Two flights of steps at the sides bring one up to the next level, and the whole outline of the palace comes into full view again. This game of alternating viewpoints is repeated in the stepped waterfall in the centre of the upper garden. Ingenious garden design, with terraces, cascades and steps, frames the architecture as if it were the backcloth of a stage set.

'Hildenbrandt's brilliant achievement lies in his organisation of all the spatial units and in transforming the terrain's natural features into levels, ramps, steps, basins and plastic groups to create a centrally concentrated external architecture on an entirely visual basis carried to a degree of perfection unrivalled in Austrian baroque art.' (Grimschitz)

The Würzburg Residence

The Würzburg Residence is an example *in excelsis* of the seat of a German prince-bishop. It marks the highest and final peak in the history of a family that began in a fairly small way but through adroit family policy, at least on the intellectual side, pushed itself to the very forefront of society. The Schönborns, whose not very extensive estates lay in Westerwald, always saw to it that their children had as good an education as possible and did not waste their time with the frivolous amusements in which most of the landed gentry spent their days. The family's rise lifted it above the stations in life usually open to those of their rank, in this case run-of-the-mill clerical benefices and livings. Before long one of the clan became a member of the cathedral chapter, then a Schönborn rose to episcopal rank in Mainz. Relations wore the mitre in Würzburg and Bamberg. By tradition the archbishopric of Mainz carried with it the highest position in the State, that of Archchancellor. So it came about that in the first third of the 18th century practically every important ecclesiastical or worldly office from the Rhine to the Danube and from Mainz to Vienna was in the hands of a Schönborn.

For the Schönborns intercourse with artists, writers and architects was an everyday matter. Although they kept their social distance, they were on cordial, almost friendly terms with some of the most remarkable figures in the artistic and intellectual world of their time. Thus they acquired a far greater knowledge of architecture and building than was usual among contemporary dilletantes. The celebrated, almost notorious Schönborn building mania bore fruit in monumental and artistically outstanding creations the size and magnificence of which were far beyond the family's means, and yet were solidly financed. Like all climbers, they had learnt to calculate. No contractor could charge them more than the job was worth. That some members of the family found ingenious methods of financing their passion for construction is testified by the actions of Johann Phillipp Franz, Count of Schönborn (1673–1724), soon after he attained the see of Würzburg. Needing money to build a new palace, it occurred to him to check the book-keeping of one of his predecessor's head officials. The new Prince Bishop was soon in possession of such explosive material that the corrupt official had to choose between a long term of imprisonment or a fine of 600,000 gulden. He decided on the latter. The successful financier, delighted with his lucky coup, exclaimed, 'Now we can set to building with a will. The Bishop of Herbipolis (Würzburg) has found a treasure!' The Schönborn correspondence on the subject of building, both between themselves and with their master builders, gives us a wonderful insight into the architectural and artistic worlds of the day and is an inexhaustible source of information for architectural historians.

159

Until the Schönborns arrived the Bishops of Würzburg had to be content with a residence inside the medieval Maria Fortress high above the town, where, in troubled times such as the peasants' revolt of the 16th century, the rulers could take refuge from their own subjects. All that was available to the bishop in the town itself were small, old-fashioned, uncomfortable quarters without any grandeur at all. To a Schönborn that was spur enough to turn the dismal lodging into something infinitely better without delay. In Balthasar Neumann, whom the bishop appointed Director of Building to the Prince Bishop in 1719, he found an architect who knew how to satisfy even a Schönborn's demand for princely display. However, far from leaving the undertaking entirely to his master builder, the Bishop was in constant contact with his family on the subject, and they in turn consulted their personal architects, who showered the prince with alternative plans and suggestions for the new palace. Even that was not enough. The Bishop now sent his master builder to study in Vienna and Paris, after which it occurred to him to send the latest plans to the most famous architects of the day, Fischer von Erlach and Hildebrandt in Vienna, and de Cotte and Boffrand in Paris, to give their opinions and produce alternative designs. To Neumann fell the thankless task of considering, sifting and integrating into his own scheme the most divers collection of architectural ideas. That he succeeded in this apparently impossible enterprise without detracting from the building's unity says much for his extraordinary ability and his gift for assimilating the extraneous—to say nothing of his tact. So it is at the same time true and yet false to assert—as is so often done in the literature of art history—that the Würzburg Residence is a product of 'collective planning'. The credit of transforming a host of contradictory, nationally oriented, high-flown, stylistically incompatible suggestions into an integrated, indigenous work of art in his own unmistakeable handwriting belongs entirely to Neumann.

Balthasar Neumann's rise to the position of Schönborn's chief architect, Director of Building—Dictator of Building, as some have called him—started from a firm foundation of craftsmanship, not all of it closely connected to architecture, but to which he remained true for the rest of his life. Born in Bohemia in 1697, the son of a weaver, he first served an apprenticeship in bell and metal casting. That knowledge came in useful later when he ran a tin foundry for the purpose of decorating Würzburg Palace. The second stage in his education was an apprenticeship as a cannon founder, followed by training as a gunsmith. Resolutely he rounded off his training by qualifying as a 'field and technical bombardment expert', which in 1712 enabled him to become a non-commissioned officer in the territorial artillery. In 1714 he entered the service of the cathedral chapter, and four years later fought in the Turkish War as a lieutenant of engineers. In 1719 he rose from the rank of Chief Engineer to become the Prince Bishop's Director of Building. It was between 1723 and 1730 that his eminent employer sent him on the above-mentioned journeys to Paris and Vienna, the rival centres of European baroque architecture, to study and to meet the leading architects.

Neumann was a building contractor in the modern sense, in that his activities were not limited to Würzburg. He maintained well organized building and planning offices under deputies in other parts of the Schönborn territory. His deputies included Engineer-lieutenant Michael Küschel in Bamberg and Neumann's pupil, Johannes Seiz in Trier. As was customary at the time, he was also responsible for road building and dyke construction, bridges and military installations. To increase his income, he used his position as contractor to add to his profit from the Würzburg Residence by establishing a glassworks to supply mirrors for the palace apartments.

Plans were begun during the reign of Johann Philipp Franz, Count of Schönborn, who, as Prince Bishop of Würzburg and Duke of Franconia, laid the foundation stone in 1720. His successors in office, Freiherr von Hutten, and his nephew, Friedrich Karl von Schönborn, State Vice Chancellor from 1704 and bishop of Würzburg after 1729, carried the project forwards, though with varying enthusiasm. By 1744 the outer walls were completed, but the interior was not yet ready. The internal decorations, finally accomplished between 1752 and 1753, reached a peak of perfection in the frescoes of Giovanni Battista Tiepolo, making the state rooms of the palace the most beautiful in late baroque architecture of Germany.

The palace, 170 metres long by 90 metres wide, consists of two wing-blocks, each containing two inner courtyards. The wing-blocks are united by the main building, the central pavilion that houses the grand staircase and the principal rooms of state. As usual in baroque palaces, the architectural formation provides the building with two decorative façades of different shape and appearance. In the front the stepped wings project far enough to form the sides of a deep forecourt. On the park side (pl. 59) there is a wide frontage extending along middle and end sections, richly varied with decorative features in high relief. Set slightly forwards, the middle section also stands out from the rest of the 170-metre-long façade by its surface being more richly accented than the simpler end façades, by its rows of double columns marking the central pavilion, and by having an extra storey with a different roof treatment. An unusual feature is the half-storey (mezzanine) inserted above the ground-floor and distinguished on the outside by a row of small, square windows. At the top of the projecting central façade is the richly decorated attic structure rising a whole storey above the rest of the top floor and crowned by a balustrade that not only completes the vertical lines, but also forms a horizontal connection between the central and wing sections.

The dominating central pavilion contains the most important rooms in the whole vast edifice: the grand staircase, the *Kaisersaal* (Imperial Hall), the *Weisser Saal* (white drawing-room) and the *sala terrena* or garden room. The visitor approaches the impressive building down the straight drive in line with the main axis, through the forecourt and into a great entrance hall (pl. 60), big enough to turn a coach-and-four in. Here the direct line the visitor has been following makes a right-angled turn, then curves round again bringing him or her to the ground floor with its five column-bordered naves. The rather oppressive vestibule, coolly, almost classically decorated, gives little idea of the glories that await the newcomer. Suddenly the low-slung central colonnade opens out into the vaulted expanse of the stair-well, from which a broad flight of stairs leads up to a midway landing, then doubles back on itself in two parallel flights on each side. The present-day visitor must decide which staircase to ascend, a choice that was no problem in the etiquette-ridden world of the 18th century. Both flights lead to a wide landing facing an anteroom. With yet another change of direction one reaches the end and climax of the journey, the chief state room.

Balthasar Neumann's stair well, enormously big for those days, has a volume of 1,200 cubic metres, a height and breadth only made possible by his ingenious construction of the roof. Owing to its great size daylight can reach the stairs from more than one direction and the airy effect is increased by Tiepolo's illusionist fresco on the cove-vaulted ceiling appearing to open it up to the heavens.

The theatrical interplay of contrasts and surprises in the Würzburger staircase was not all to be found in the architect's original conception. Instead of the present classicist decoration, Neumann had planned something more

Pages 162–163:

78 *Pommersfelden, Weissenstein Palace: the Marble Room. Completed in its raw state in 1715, the Marble Room impresses above all by the marble columns and pilasters that adorn its high walls. Their architraves support arches that are alternately rounded and doubly voluted. Framed wall paintings by the Austrian artist Johann Franz Michael Rottmayr (1717) represent 'Wisdom and Clear Conscience triumphing over Vice'. Above them stretches the ceiling fresco by Daneil Schenks. The decor is completed by a floor of red, grey and black marble tiles (1718).*

79 *Pommersfelden, Weissenstein Palace: the Mirror Cabinet. Splendour and extravagance are not confined to the state rooms but extend to the smaller private apartments of the palace, especially those of Lothar Franz von Schönborn. The costliest, most splendid and most perfectly maintained of all the baroque interior decoration is to be found in the Pommersfelden Mirror Cabinet. Franz Lothar introduced this type of room, first developed by the Dutch in the late 17th century, into German palace architecture. His first mirror-lined room, installed at Schloss Gaibach, he designed himself, but he left the planning and execution of the one at Pommersfelden (1710–1718) to his master-carpenter, Ferdinand Plitzner. The carved panelling and wonderfully inlaind floor show Plitzner to have been one of the most accomplished artist-carpenters of the baroque era. His style reflects influences from both Vienna and France. The current taste for the exotic accounts for the chinoiserie of the decorative patterns and for the valuable oriental pottery displayed beside and above the mirrors and on the console tables. Another theme is chosen for the carved figures on the doors, which portray characters from the Commedia dell'Arte as grotesques. The central oval of the floor inlay is repeated in the middle of the gold-framed ceiling. Six more looking-glasses are set in the cove-vaulting, alternating with gilded medallions showing the deeds of Hercules and Apollo in low relief.*

rococo and relaxed, including the opening up of the walls beside the staircases to give a feeling of spaciousness and glimpses of columns and arches as in the palace of the Archbishop of Trier designed between 1757 and 1758 by his pupil F. Dietz. But none of the later changes and additions could alter the heart of Neumann's plan, namely to displace the principal state room as the one dominating centre of the palace by promoting the staircase from a purely functional means of communication to a work of architecture in its own right.

M. H. V. Freeden considered that the 'magnificent staircase at Würzburg is really the chief state apartment'.

The present decorative stuccowork was carried out by Ludovico Bossi after Neumann's death. It adorns the walls of the upper part in the shape of pilaster capitals and of *putti* with vases and emblems above the panels and doorways. From the prominent cornice over-lifesize pairs of figures appear to support the weight of the ceiling. Statues in the round adorn banisters and landing balustrade. Allegorical and mythological figures, cherubs, vases and lampholders break the balustrade's straight line. Figures in groups representing the Four Seasons, Meleager and Atalanta, Apollo and Paris, 'Midday' and 'Evening', populate the stair well. Over this world of mythology and allegory curves the famous ceiling painting done between 1752 and 1753 by Giovanni Battista Tiepolo in honour of the Prince Bishop Philip von Greiffenclau. Paying homage to their patron are the 'Four Corners of the Earth', 'Europa with her Bull', 'Music' and 'Art'. Generously, the bishop allowed Balthasar to be included in the painting, dressed in colonel's uniform and sitting on a cannon. Often the fresco painters themselves, Tiepolo among them, were represented as joining the whole earth, personified as 'Asia', 'Europe', and so on, in painted homage to the ruler. The illusive skies are peopled, too, with all the gods of Olympus.

After the intoxicating splendour of the staircase, it is hard to think of anything to cap its effect. And so the designer has resorted to the typically baroque scenic stratagem of contrast. The next room we come to is the exquisite but cooler, more temperate White Drawing Room (also known as the *Salle des Gardes*). The *crescendo* of the staircase drops to the *piano* of a room decorated in shades of off-white to prepare us for the feast of colour and magnificence in the adjacent *Kaisersaal*. In the White Drawing Room (pl. 64) there is no gilding or polychromatic fresco, only the white, shading to palest blue, of walls and ceiling. These, however, are adorned with the most delicate, graceful stuccowork, a masterpiece wrought by the Lugano plasterer Antonio Bossi in 1744. The swirls of rococo shells and foliage are interspersed with emblems of War (hence *Salle d'Armes*), insignia of nobility, flying cherubs and more dignified figures such as Mars and Bellona, now in Arcadian pastoral guise. Darker notes in the subtle colour scheme are the brown doors with lighter brown frames inset with reddish brown marble panels, the black iron stove, the grey marble overmantel and the dark brown console table. The whole elegant, lacey composition was completed in only a few months.

The White Drawing Room, however, is only an anteroom to relax the visitor before entering the glorious climax and ceremonial heart of the palace. Colourful door hangings introduce us to the next apartment, known from its high purpose as the *Kaisersaal*, or Emperor's Room (pl. 62). Facing the park, the chief of a suite of state rooms, this ceremonial hall seems to be the gathering place of all the creative gifts of a far from talentless era. Balthasar Neumann and Tiepolo between them made this into one of the most superlative spatial compositions of European baroque design. The bare brickwork was ready in 1741, but the decoration could not be started, because during the reign of Friedrich Carl von Schönborn there was not enough money available. The work was completed during the years 1749–1753 under Carl Philipp von Greiffenclau. The new Prince Bishop, not wishing to be less munificent in his patronage than his Schönborn predecessors, arranged for the greatest fresco-painter of the age, the Venetian Giovanni Battista Tiepolo, to come to Würzburg on the most princely terms, and entrusted him not only with the ceiling decoration over the grand staircase, but also the frescoes in the *Kaisersaal*.

The domed, oblong-octagonal hall is situated in the centre of the palace, rising from first floor to roof. It is demarcated by three-quarter, marble columns along the walls. Above the powerful main cornice soars the lofty, nearly oval cupola. The structural framework with its clear division of supporting and supported parts, the columns and cupola, is echoed in the forms and colours of the decoration, giving the room its unique quality. The colour scheme is set by the agate-coloured marble, flecked with blue and gold, that spreads out from the paving, skirting and pedestals to the walls. The spaces between the columns are enlivened by the greenish yellow of the inset panels and marble chimneypiece. White marble figures and panels lighten the subdued colour scheme, the whole forming a neutral background for the glowing colours of the frescoes and the rich gilding of the ornamentation. The golden swirls of decoration play endless variations on that favourite rococo theme, the scallop shell, curling round the wall panels, the ribs of the vaulting and the capitals of the columns, framing the window recesses and pictures, encrusting coats of arms above the doorways.

The crowning glory of the whole exuberant display, with all its precious materials, is the ceiling painted by Tiepolo. The subject is 'The Wedding of Emperor Barbarossa and Beatrice of Burgundy'. The historical event is elevated to the mythological sphere of the Olympian gods. In the lower part of the fresco the bridal coach, drawn by the horses of Apollo, brings the princess to the enthroned emperor. The wedding itself, solemnized by the Bishop of Würzburg, brings in the local connection. To underline the importance of the occasion to the spiritual and worldly authority of the bishopric, another crowded scene celebrates Barbarossa's confirmation of the Bishop of Würzburg's claim to the Dukedom of Franconia. It also identifies the Empire as the source and legitimation of power. Through the historical incident, blurred though it is by its mythological aura, an actual political relationship, namely the close bond between the Schönborns and the imperial court in Vienna, is fortified and, through the medium of art, given perpetual validity.

The Palace of Pommersfelden

'This building business is diabolical. Once you start you can't stop. ...' Lothar Franz, Count von Schönborn, Prince Bishop of Bamberg and Elector of Mainz admitted in a letter. Infected with that devilish building bug even more virulently than the rest of his construction-mad family, the Prince Bishop, already responsible for the palaces of Gaibach and Favorite, announced in November 1711 that he had 'just started building a very big palace in Pommersfelden'. Lothar Franz von Schönborn was born in Aschaffenburg in the year 1655. After his studies in Vienna and a successful stint as a capitular of Bamberg and Würzburg Cathedrals he was elected to the see of Bamberg in 1693. Two years later his career culminated in the highest and most influential ecclesiastical post in the whole Empire: he became Archbishop of Mainz, and therewith Prince Elector and Imperial Lord Chancellor. He had a deciding voice in the election of Charles VI. The

successful candidate rewarded his princely Primate with the not inconsiderable sum of 100,000 guilders, which Lothar Franz used as a building fund for his Pommersfelden palace.

In 1710 Lothar Franz inherited the estate of Pommersfelden. The old moated castle of the former Lord High Stewards of Pommersfelden proving unsuitable for expansion, he started on a brand-new palace. The planning of the projected mansion, intended originally as a family seat, was entrusted in 1711 to Johann Dientzenhofer (1663–1721), an architect who had studied in Bohemia and proved his worth in the building of Fulda Cathedral. The Prince Bishop appointed him Chief Master Builder of Bamberg. He designed the palace (built between 1711 and 1716) in the form of a horseshoe made up of four wing sections on either side of a huge middle block. The whole three storeys of this central part are taken up by a grand staircase which owes something to the Viennese architect Lukas von Hildebrandt. He worked in close collaboration with his patron, who was well versed in every branch of contemporary architecture. The connection between Pommersfelden and Hildebrandt came about naturally enough, since Lothar Franze's nephew, Friedrich Karl von Schönborn, being the vice-Chancellor, lived in Vienna and employed Hildebrandt there as his personal architect. Thus Hildebrandt was well qualified to give advice on the subject, and over a hundred Schönborn letters between Vienna and Bamberg still exist to testify to this remarkable exchange of architectural knowledge.

On the ground floor, behind the grand central staircase, lies the extravagantly ornamented, grottoesque garden room leading out into the now anglicised park. Above this *sala terrena* is the principal room of the palace, known from its costly décor as the Marble Room. In company with Dientzenhofer and Hildebrandt, a third architect, Maximilian von Welsch (1671–1745), should be given some credit. Between 1717 and 1718, opposite the palace's boldly projecting middle block, he built the stables, the elegant backward curve of which cleverly complements the line of the central pavilion facing it. This entrance façade (pl. 75) is distinguished by rich architectural and decorative elements. Above the rusticated ground floor two full columns frame the main entrance and, together with the pilasters at the sides, bind the two principal storeys together. The columns and corner pilasters underpin a classical pediment bearing the Schönborn coat-of-arms supported by two lions. Above the heraldic shield stands the figure of Mercury, referring perhaps to the fact that without astute financial planning no such baroque building could exist. The central pavilion jutting forwards from the massive side wings encloses the three principal domains of the palace: the staircase (pl. 76), the Marble Room (pl. 78) and the garden room (pl. 80). The basic concept of the main stairway, at that time unusually grandiose by German standards, even for a palace, came from the architect's patron, who, right from the planning stage had consulted his nephew, the Vice-Chancellor in Vienna. Thus, from the beginning the plans worked out by Dientzenhofer were submitted to Hildebrandt, whose superior genius the Bishop of Bamberg acknowledged, on condition his basic idea for the staircase was left intact. 'My stairs must remain;' he stipulated, 'they are my invention and my masterpiece'. Hildebrandt worked out the arrangement of the central pavilion with the help of rough sketches sent from Pommersfelden. The main concept was of symmetrical flights of steps leading up to a gallery in front of the principal state apartment. The immense space taken up by the stair well forced Hildebrandt to extend the central block far forwards into the forecourt. On the final plans sent in 1713 he wrote, '... climbing the triple flight of stairs one arrives at the *étage noble* where an encircling walk

81 *Blenheim Palace: view of the English-style landscaped grounds designed by the famous landscape gardener 'Capability' Brown between 1764 and 1765 in the new fashion of romantic sentiment and picturesque effect, thus some 20 years before the park of the Petit Trianon in Versailles was anglicised. The seemingly natural park is in charming contrast to the theatrical magnificence of Blenhiem Palace built in the truly baroque style of the early eighteenth century. Brown dammed the little river Glyme, running through the Woodstock estate, to form a seemingly natural lake, leaving a picturesque island in the middle with graceful groups of trees and shrubs. He also integrated Vanbrugh's much older baroque bridge into his new romantic landscape. The composition of lake, island and trees is reminiscent of the park scenery of Jean-Jacques Rousseau's retreat in Ermenonville where he died in 1778. The new fashion in gardens may have been influenced by the love of nature and 'sensibility' propounded in his seminal works* Emile *and* The New Heloïse, *which appeared in 1761 and 1762, shortly before Brown came to Blenheim. It is a pity that the plan to preserve the remains of the Elizabethan manor house (destroyed in Cromwell's time) on the estate fell through. Picturesque ruins were so much in demand as park attractions at the time that artificial ones were often erected.*

supported on columns will break up the all too spacious stair-well into the correct proportions, while an open gallery above will maintain communications between the two storeys'.

Judging from the exchange of letters on the subject, the respective contributions of the patron and his architect can be summed up as follows: Lothar Franz von Schönborn planned the double flight of stairs which Lucas von Hildebrandt set in a two-storeyed arcade system surrounded with galleries and columns.

It was a new type of stair-well that both created and solved problems. Clearly derived from the exterior galleried courtyard, though no longer recognizable as such, it took up so much room that either the whole structure had to be greatly reduced in size or the frontage of the building radically altered in ground plan. In the first case it could not be adequately lit during the day; in the second case daylight could enter from three sides. Another problem solved by the arcade design entirely due to Hildebrandt was the easy accessibility of all the surrounding rooms.

That even the French architects of the time, who had hitherto been critical of the opulent German staircases, could not deny the splendid effect of Hildebrandt's creation is clear from the opinion expressed by the 'pope of French architecture', Germain Boffrand. On seeing Pommersfelden, he exclaimed *'Je suis frappé d'étonnement car d'on ne voit rien de pareil, de si magnifique dans toute la France'* (I am astonished. Nothing so magnificent is to be seen in the whole of France).

Blenheim Palace

Together with Castle Howard and a few other ducal residences, Blenheim Palace represents the English contribution to the art of palace-building in baroque Europe. Neither in artistic quality nor in sheer size do they lag behind the French and Austro–German examples. Blenheim Palace covers an area of 275 by 175 metres. However, when one turns to the patrons who commissioned those works and acted as artistic impresarios in their production, the difference and divergent development of England is striking. She had escaped, both politically and socially, the absolutism that dominated most of Europe at that time. The builder of this grandest of English baroque palaces was not the king, nor even one of the ruling class, but the most important general of his time and nation, the Duke of Marlborough. To reward the Duke for his extraordinary military ability, which had had a decisive effect in the final confrontation with France, Queen Anne recommended Parliament to grant him the large estate of Woodstock and a sum of 240,000 pounds to build a suitable house.

Nominally, the sum was lent, not given, in token of which the holder of the title must to this day pay annual interest to the crown in the shape of a silk flag.

The palace's name of Blenheim comes from the Swabian village of Blindheim where, in the year 1704 Marlborough together with Prince Eugene of Savoy inflicted a crushing defeat (16,000 dead, twice as many wounded and 11,000 prisoners) on Louis XIV's army, thus ending the War of the Spanish Succession and destroying the myth of the *Grande Armée*'s invincibility.

The principle architect, John Vanbrugh (1664–1726), was also an unusual personality when compared to his counterparts on the continent. The son of a confectioner of Flemish extraction, he started life as a soldier. Arrested in Calais in 1690 as an English spy, he spent two years in the Bastille, and during

82 *Blenheim Palace: view of the entrance façade in front of the Great Hall, showing the display side of the mansion facing the large forecourt. Blenheim was a memorial to the battle fought at Hochstadt-Blindheim in 1704, when Louis XIV's army was decisively beaten by the combined forces of the Duke of Marlborough and Prince Eugene of Savoy. Presented to the Duke by Queen Anne and a grateful nation, the palace (1705–1724) was first designed by John Vanbrugh, then continued under Nicholas Hawksmoor. The building is the most important and extensive work of baroque palace architecture in the English style. Our illustration gives some impression of the magnificence and monumentality of the mansion, with its four wings and five courtyards, and also of its artistic sources: classical Antiquity, the Middle Ages and the Renaissance. Visible on the left of the picture is one of the turrets so reminiscent of medieval castles and Elizabethan manor houses. The architecture of the grand portico with its pediment, columns and pillars on the formidable projecting front of the main block reminds one in its regularity of ancient Greek and Roman buildings, or of the works and projects of the important late Renaissance designers, Palladio and Scamozzi, whose architectural doctrines had great influence in 18th century England. A complicated arrangement of steps leads from forecourt to entrance portico in the Palladian county-house manner.*

83 *Blenhiem Palace: the Great Hall in the middle axis of the building. The creator of this coolly classical entrance hall was John Vanbrugh. The hall carries on the monumental style of the portico, especially in its now fluted Corinthian columns supporting the surrounding cornice. Leading up to the* vaulting, *in which a fresco glorifies Marlborough's victory of 1704, there are bas-reliefs of antique weapons and trophies, referring to the palace's military origin. Some French flags captured at Blenheim form part of the decoration. When one views the Hall's cold and lofty magnificence one can under-* stand that Voltaire felt uncomfortable there when on a visit, and appreciate Alexander Pope's mocking verse:

    'Thanks, Sir, cry'd I, 'tis very fine. But where d'ye sleep, or where d'ye dine? I find by all you have been telling, That 'tis a house, but not a dwelling.'

84 *Blenheim Palace: the chapel. Memorial put up by Sarah Churchill for her husband, John, Duke of Marlborough. William Kent (1685–1748), the famous English architect, painter, decorator and landscape gardener was responsible for the design, which was executed by Rysbrack. In form and content the memorial is of the usual late baroque type often seen in France, Germany, Austria and Italy. In front of a dark green, marble background in the shape of an ancient obelisk stands the Duke dressed, as befits his profession, as a victorious emperor with laurel wreath and field marshal's baton, his sandalled foot resting on an antique helmet. At his side, in a Roman type of chair and dressed in flowing robes and a stylised coronet, sits the Duchess, her younger son by her knee, the elder at his father's side. The portrait heads are somewhat idealized. At the feet of the family group lies the Duke's voluted sarcophagus in dark red marble supporting two allegorical figures. On the picture's right Fame sits ready to proclaim Marlborough's heroic deeds with a fanfare; on the left History with a quill pen writes an inscription in the book of remembrance: 'To the memory of John, Duke of Marlborough and his two sons, Sarah his Duchess has erected this monument in the year of Christ MDCCXXXIII'. Sarah Churchill, born in 1660, survived her husband, the Duke (1650–1722) by more than twenty years.*

84

175

his imprisonment began to write plays. On his return to England he achieved a considerable success with his comedies of manners, which still appear on our stage from time to time. Puritan circles attacked them for their immorality. Whether for that reason, or because of the typically British love of the outsider, the gifted amateur without formal qualifications, he next turned to architecture. In 1702, after only three years' practice, he was appointed Comptroller in the Office of Works, the royal board of architects, charged with the supervision of all public buildings. Hence his commission to design the semi-official victory memorial of Blenheim. Among other things, as Comptroller of Building he co-operated with Sir Christopher Wren, the most important architect of English high baroque and the creator of St Paul's Cathedral in London. In 1714 Vanbrugh was knighted.

Since the Duke spent most of his time moving from battlefield to battlefield and from conference to conference, Vanbrugh's real collaborator was the Duchess, Sarah Churchill. Highly intelligent and gifted with artistic sensibility though she was, Marlborough's wife was also temperamental, hard to please, miserly and suspicious. She made life difficult for Vanbrugh, for his 1,500-odd building artisans and for the Duke, who supervised operations from a distance and whom she pursued over half Europe with a stream of progress reports in letter form. In 1716 Vanbrugh resigned rather than have further dealings with his quarrelsome patroness, and handed over the commission to his collaborator of long standing, the professional architect Nicholas Hawksmoor (1661–1735). Among the projects that fell victim to Sarah's frugality were a spectacular bridge over the Glyme river and a fashionable scheme of Vanbrugh's to preserve the abandoned Elizabethan palace in the grounds, devastated by Cromwell's troops, as a picturesque ruin. In spite of these continual arguments and frustrations, the result we see today is magnificent enough and—notwithstanding the change of architects—amazingly consistent.

As a symbol in stone of England's supremacy over France (Grinling Gibbons' carvings celebrate that situation) Blenheim represents England's 'counter-culture' in relation to both France and the continental version of baroque. The artistic and formal sources lie in the antique world, in the late Italian Renaissance with such architects as Palladio and his great pupil Scamozzi (whose treatises had long been translated into English and were eagerly exploited) and also in the English late Middle Ages and the golden Elizabethan Renaissance.

The layout is many-winged and monumental, with striking three-dimensional values, planned above all for its effect in the landscape and from a distance. The centrally situated residential part of the building, with views on every side like an Italian renaissance palace or villa, has a substantial wing attached to each of its four corners. Each wing is crowned with a peculiar, challenging tower reminiscent of medieval or Tudor country mansions, giving the palace a typically English appearance. One could search the continent in vain for a comparable feature built in the 17th or 18th century. The frontages of both side-wings curve forward into a semi-circular shape resembling the exedra of ancient Roman baths. In front, two complete out-buildings, the stables and kitchen quarters, stretch forward, making two sides of the huge forecourt.

The whole rambling complex, with its covered terraces, low connecting colonnades, inner courtyards, the great central block containing the huge entrance hall and state rooms, the chapel beside the stable wing, and the greenhouses by the kitchen courtyard, reminds one of Palladio's space-gobbling designs for Italian noblemen's villas, or his imaginary recon-

85 *Blenheim Palace: the Saloon, situated in the centre of the house, directly behind the Great Hall, is used to this day as a banqueting hall on festive occasions. As befitting a great villa set in open country, the room is surrounded with sumptuous* trompe d'oeil *frescos suggesting a hall with views of a fantastic outside world on all sides. Huge square openings hung with painted draperies and framed by tall painted columns look out on to a cloud-decked summer sky. Half-length figures leaning over the parapet as if looking at the inside of the room increase the effect of deep perspective. This type of decoration, never found on the continent in the 18th century, shows how differently baroque architecture – both exterior and interior – developed in England. It was much more closely related to works of late Italian renaissance architects such as Palladio, who were high fashion in 18th century England, perhaps due to the effects of the Grand Tour. Painters of the school of Paolo Veronese and Zelotti produced frescos of this type in Italian villas of the late 16th century.*

86 *London, Buckingham Palace: the residence of British monarchs in the capital, though only since the reign of Queen Victoria (1837–1901). The house was originally built for the Duke of Buckingham in 1703, but passed into the possession of George III in 1762. A few years after radical rebuilding in 1825 by the famous neo-classical architect John Nash, Queen Victoria adopted it as her London palace. Nash's work was fashionable in the highest social circles; his talent was versatile but sometimes superficial. One of the most prominent representatives of the historical trend in neo-classical architecture, he was nevertheless not averse to the exotic, as in the Islamic borrowings of the Royal Pavilion at Brighton. The façade of Buckingham Palace, however, is regular, canonical and devoid of all excitement. That was not the fault of the architect but of the taste of high society in the early 19th century. The justly celebrated terraces surrounding Regent's Park are also the work of this architect. In the foreground of the photograph is the Queen Victoria Memorial, imposing in its size, erected in our own century.*

87 *Chatsworth House, Derbyshire. This palace in the form of a glorified country house is set in extensive, typically English parkland that appears completely natural, although it was originally a carefully calculated picturesque composition. It was built at the turn of the 17th to 18th century (1687–1706) for the first Duke of Devonshire, but was not completed till the 19th century. In its cool, almost classical, elegance it is reminiscent of the country chateaux of contemporary France. The strongly accented attic storey with its attractive balustrade and superimposed urns certainly resembles that of French country seats, although the steeply inclined roof favoured by Mansart and his followers is missing. However, the central entrance façade in which colossal fluted ionic half-columns support a triangular pediment adorned with bas-reliefs and surmounted by a classical figure show a more Italian influence. Italian Renaissance architects such as Palladio and Scamozzi could not have designed it with more classical regularity. Although built in the same canonical spirit as the entrance façade and portico of Blenheim, here the conception is less plastic and more two-dimensional. In its size, splendour and beauty this princely – almost royal – seat bears witness to the undisputed pretensions of the English nobility who were the ruling classes in the 17th and 18th centuries. The rejection of the 'French' and 'baroque' architecture that expressed the spirit of absolutism, and the return to Palladio's classicism explain the contrast between the regular and axial conformation of the great country houses and the free world of their landscaped parks that followed no architectural rules and axes. The visitor from continental Europe, accustomed to the sight of Versailles, Belvedere or Schönbrunn, finds this antithesis between architectural reason (the palace) and natural unreason (the gardens) as delightful as it is unusual and illogical. To English philosophy and artistic theory, however, there was no contradiction there, far more a perfect accord. Palladio's architecture, on which the neo-classical style was based, was rational, functional and hence 'natural': in other words as far removed as possible from French and baroque building. The equation of nature and reason was extended to garden design. In the name of reason and enlightenment, therefore, only a natural, free, English, landscaped park was rational and aesthetic. Since unnaturalness and irrationality were equated, we can understand Addison's saying 1712 – about the time Blenheim and Chatsworth were built – that he would rather see a tree in all the wealth of its leaves and branches than twisted into a geometrical figure. Thus the political rejection of French absolutism and Stuart attempts to seize absolute power was transformed beyond recognition into an artistic policy.*

structions of the massive and ramified buildings of ancient Rome, such as baths, fora or palaces, found in his '*Quattro Libri*' of 1570. The main entrance façade with its triangular pediment supported on colossal Corinthian columns and pilasters is a regularly classical 'frontispiece' of majestic and centralizing power such as Palladio himself could not have bettered. Its dramatic contrasts of light and shadow recall the spirit of the 16th century far more than that of the 18th (pl. 82). The monumental effect of the whole is enhanced by the great English park laid out by the famous landscape gardener 'Capability' Brown (1764–65). Neither extending the plan of the mansion nor formally leading up to it in the French style, the seemingly natural, though cunningly designed, parkland runs up to its walls in attractive contrast. Brown dammed the little river to form a 'natural' lake with island and bridge; he arranged lawns, ornamental waters, undulations and picturesque groups of trees to compose an ideal landscape painting in the grand manner. In our own century Charles, ninth Duke of Marlborough, partly restored the original French formal gardens by laying out a terraced water garden beside the library wing.

Among the enormous crowds that visit Blenheim Palace in the holiday season, there are many that come on pilgrimages to see the place where Sir Winston Churchill, grandson of the seventh Duke, coming rather too hastily into the world, was born in a spare bedroom during a party in 1874. He was always fond of Blenheim and visited it frequently. It was there that he proposed marriage, and it is in the churchyard of the little village church of nearby Bladon that his mortal remains were laid to rest.

88 *Brighton, Royal Pavilion. The chief creator of this strangest and almost facetious aristocratic residence in England was John Nash, fashionable architect to the nobility, who a few years later (1825) reconstructed Buckingham Palace for the king. Brighton Pavilion in its present form was built for George IV when he was Prince Regent. The basic idea, namely to make a royal summer villa in exotic, oriental shapes, may have been in the air even when the original building was erected (from 1784 onwards). It may have been an extension of the fancy for exotic pavilions and romantic ruins as decorations in English parks, or even in some French gardens of the baroque period. At Schwetzinger Palace, for instance, where the park was 'anglicized' in the late 18th century, the designer Sckell adorned it with a fantastic mosque. Here, in the less official and ceremonial atmosphere of a pleasure and summer palace by the sea, Nash could give his imagination free rein. As a historicist he turned to themes not only far removed in time, but also in distance. So arose a strange mixture from Arabian, Islamic, Persian and Chinese sources and from the India of the Mogul emperors. Contemporaries were fascinated by what they called the 'Hindu manner', or Indian Gothic, referring to the prettified Gothic revival in English architecture and gardens of the 18th and early 19th centuries. With the Royal Pavilion Nash started the masquerade of revivals and borrowings that ransacked every possible period of history and land of origin. As early as 1809 a hamlet of 'old English' thatched, timber-frame cottages had been built in the grounds of Blaise Castle House in frank imitation of Marie Antoinette's* Le Hameau *at Versailles. An extra link between India and a royal English residence lay in the sub-continent's increasing annexation by Britain, which reached its climax when Queen Victoria was proclaimed Empress of India in the late 19th century. Thus a feeling for Indian architecutre and culture was brought to England from her Far Eastern colonies. The typically English love of eccentricity and the unusual introduced this architectual caprice into the not very numerous category of 'humorous buildings'.*

89

89 *Leningrad, the Winter Palace: the Palace Square frontage. Some 50 years after Peter the Great founded the new capital his modest Government House was replaced by the vast Winter Palace (1754–1762). It was designed by the Architect-in-Chief to the Imperial Court, Count Bartolomeo Francesco Rastrelli (1700–1771) who since 1730, had worked in St Petersburg, and reached the peak of his artistic career during the reign of Empress Elizabeth (1741–1761). Trained in Paris, and familiar with the best buildings of Germany, Austria and Italy, he had at his fingertips the whole of European baroque architecurre. With the widespread eclecticism of the time, he integrated into his creations stylistic elements from the early, high and late Baroque as well as the Rococo period. The result is a mixture of baroque massiveness and easy rococo grace.*

Pages 184–185:
90 *Leningrad, Michael Palace: In Russia, after the death of Catherine II, the stage of the so-called Alexandrinian Empire (1796–1840) set in. Alexander I wanted to make St Petersburg into a capital city of the western type. Among the leading architects who helped the Tzar to realize his ambitious plans, Carlo di Rossi took first place. His creations, inspired by antiquity, blended the ancient Greek and Roman into a style all his own. A food example is the interior of the Michael Palace, built 1819–1823, which since 1898 has housed the Russian Museum. The room is characterized by its restrained colouring, mostly concentrated in the ceiling area, while walls and columns are left pure white.*

91 *Tzarskoe Selo (today called Pushkin),*
the Great Palace: Between 1752 and 1757, on
the orders of the Empress Elizabeth, Rastrelli
converted a small palace into an enormous
one. In so doing, however, he had to observe
her expressed wish to preserve as much as
possible of Peter the Great's former residence.
In this pious treasuring of a father's heritage
the modern cult for conserving ancient monu-
ments is already apparent. To the three-
storeyed main block with its short lateral
wings Rastrelli added extensions several times
longer than the original facade, creating a
frontage 300 metres long. The façade ends in
right-angled pavilions. In the left-hand pav-
ilion is the palace chapel under a roof adorned
with five copper cupolas. That form of roofing
belonged to old Russia and symbolizes the
historical spirit of the time, which saw nothing
incongruous in combinig the latest baroque
forms with traditional elements from the
repertory of historical Russian architecture.